Obeying the Great Commission

Additional books by Dr. Wilkins.
Scan the QR Code to view, or visit www.jameswilkins.org

Obeying the Great Commission

Equipping You for Your New Vocation

Teach prior to the *Personal Growth Seminar*

Dr. James Wilkins

LIFE SENTENCE
Publishing, LLC

www.lifesentencepublishing.com

Visit Dr. Wilkins' website: www.jameswilkins.org

Obeying the Great Commission – Dr. James Wilkins

Copyright © 2014

Scripture quotations are taken from the Holy Bible, King James Version, Cambridge, 1769.

Printed in the United States of America

First edition published 2014

LIFE SENTENCE Publishing books are available at discounted prices for ministries and other outreach. Find out more by contacting info@lifesentencepublishing.com

LIFE SENTENCE Publishing and its logo are trademarks of

LIFE SENTENCE Publishing, LLC
P.O. Box 652
Abbotsford, WI 54405

Paperback ISBN: 978-1-62245-170-8

Ebook ISBN: 978-1-62245-171-5

10 9 8 7 6 5 4 3 2 1

This book is available from Amazon.com, Barnes & Noble, and your local Christian bookstore.

Cover Design: Amber Burger

Editor: Mary Vesperman, Ruth Zetek

Share this book on Facebook

LOVINGLY DEDICATED
TO THE ALLISONS

Katie, Age 80, And Dana, Age 87

The Allisons attended a *Personal Growth Seminar* in August 2012, and to their surprise they learned the following:

According to Ephesians 4:11, a person gets a new vocation when he is saved. Jesus clearly explained this new vocation to the apostles when He said, *Follow me and I will make you fishers of men.* Their new vocation, winning souls, was to become their primary job for the rest of their lives.

The Allisons accepted the fact that they were designed by God to reproduce themselves and win souls (Proverbs 11:30). They learned where their fears and inadequacies were coming from and how to witness with confidence.

They learned that in order to do any job, a person had **to do the job.** In order to become skilled at anything, one must practice. One learns to play the piano through hours of practice. One learns to become a good ball player through practice. **The Allisons spent hours rehearsing as they presented the four spiritual principles.**

These dear people were used of the Lord to change the eternal sufferings of four loved ones from hell to the glories and joy of heaven. They travelled many miles to win two lifelong friends, both aged 81 (who have both since died). Then it was Walter, a cousin and veteran of WWII, (also since died). Bonnie, another cousin who lived in Oregon, was led to the Lord by telephone (also since died). They have also won Dana's 91-year-old sister and others.

The Allisons' prayer is that the people who read this book will also commit to learning and doing their new vocation. The Allisons' immense joy in winning people to the Lord has already begun, but thanks to their Saviour, it will never end.

Contents

SIMPLE STEPS IN USING THIS BOOK XI

HOW TO BEGIN YOUR LESSON.................................XII

FOR ADDED BLESSINGS AND GROWTH................ XIV

RETENTION: WILL IT BE 6 Percent OR 62 Percent? ..XV

FOREWORD...XVII

LESSON ONE
THE GREAT COMMISSION WILL SOLVE THE
WORLD'S TWO GREATEST NEEDS 1

LESSON TWO
YOUR NEW VOCATION UNDER THE GREAT
COMMISSION 15

LESSON THREE
WHAT DID JESUS MEAN WHEN HE GAVE THE
GREAT COMMISSION? 30

LESSON FOUR
HOW DID THE FIRST CHURCH OBEY THE GREAT
COMMISSION IN DEVELOPING THEIR CONVERTS
INTO SOUL WINNERS?...43

LESSON FIVE
HOW AND WHY DID THE PREACHERS PERFECT
THE SAINTS? 57

LESSON SIX
OBEYING THE GREAT COMMISSION WILL BRING
NATIONAL REVIVAL 71

LESSON SEVEN
WHAT WILL HAPPEN IF WE DISOBEY THE GREAT
COMMISSION?..90

LESSON EIGHT
THE GREAT COMMISSION OFFERS HOPE FOR THE

LESSON NINE
**HOPE FOR THE PRESENT SUFFERING OF THE
DYING MASSES**..121

LESSON TEN
**THE ETERNAL SUFFERINGS OF THOSE WHOM THE
GREAT COMMISSION DID NOT REACH** 132

LESSON ELEVEN
**THE PLACE OF TEARS AND COMPASSION IN THE
GREAT COMMISSION** 153

LESSON TWELVE
**GOD'S GIFT TO PASTORS FOR OBEYING THE GREAT
COMMISSION** 173

LESSON THIRTEEN
**GOD'S GIFT TO PASTORS WHO LEAD IN OBEYING
THE GREAT COMMISSION** 188

ABOUT THE AUTHOR 207

SIMPLE STEPS IN USING THIS BOOK

1. Each adult and teen should go through these lessons in a Bible class before attending the *Personal Growth Seminar.*

2. The student goes over the *Dear Disciple* letter and fills in the blanks on the prayer list page.

3. The *Role Model* goes over the *Daily Declaration* and explains how to do it each morning and evening.

4. The *Role Model* explains the grading procedure. He explains that the new member is to read each daily assignment on the day assigned for each part of his lesson before answering any of the questions.

5. Then he is to fill in the blanks on the day designated: Monday's on Monday, Tuesday's on Tuesday, and so on. Each question is represented in the text by the symbol (*). The questions are designed to aid in the learning process.

6. Each week the *Role Model* sets up a visit at an appointed time on a Saturday or Sunday to fellowship, review, and go over the questions.

7. The *Role Model* assigns the proper grade as follows:

A = Excellent: Did the work on a daily basis.
B = Good: Did all the work, but not on a daily basis.
J = Future Judgment: Did not complete all the blanks.

8. The *Role Model* has prayer, leaves, and makes his report.

9. The same procedure is followed each week.

HOW TO BEGIN YOUR LESSON

OUR FATHER IN HEAVEN

With knowledge that the Bible commands each disciple to pray regularly and with a desire to pray more consistently in order to secure definite results make the following prayer list.

Pray for These Things:

1. **I'll pray for myself**, for a humble, submissive spirit toward Christ.
2. **For my family**, that I may be a Christian testimony and a blessing to each one of them.
3. **For my pastor**, that God will give him the grace, spiritual power, and wisdom to lead, feed, and shepherd the flock.
4. **For my country**, that God will send revival to our nation, especially to those in high positions.
5. **For our missionaries**, for their safety, success, and support. (Write down the missionaries' names and their countries.)

1. _____ country _____

2. _____ country _____

3. _____ country _____

6. **For my lost loved ones and friends**. Write down at least three people you will pray for daily.

1. _____ Date prayer answered _____

2. _____ Date prayer answered _____

3. _____ Date prayer answered _____

7. **For evangelists and other special workers**, and call them by name (James Wilkins).

How to Conclude: IN JESUS' NAME (with authority), AMEN.

FOR ADDED BLESSINGS AND GROWTH

… as he thinketh in his heart, so is he … (**Prov. 23:7**).

This verse reflects one of the greatest psycho-logical and biblical principles:

- How a person thinks is the type of person he will be.
- If one thinks negative, worldly thoughts, he will live a negative and worldly life.
- If one takes into his mind positive thoughts of faith, he will live a positive life of faith.
- One can change a poor self-image by developing good positive habits.
- One can strengthen himself and increase faith by doing three things:
    1. Majoring on good, healthy thoughts
    2. Washing one's mind by reading and memorizing Scripture
    3. Stating right objectives and positive goals

ONE CAN DEVELOP A GOOD, HAPPY INNER SELF BY THIS SIMPLE DAILY EXERCISE.

A MUST: Repeat the *Daily Declarations* at least every morning and evening.

A MUST: Strive to memorize the memory verse each week.

RETENTION: WILL IT BE 6 Percent OR 62 Percent?

Do you want to learn? It is really up to you!

These lessons were designed so you can maximize your ability to learn and remember what you have learned.

6 % If you read an article once, chances are you will not remember much about it after a period of time. The average person can recall only 6 percent of what he read just two weeks earlier.

If, however, you read the article and review it for six consecutive days, the **62 %** average rate of retention goes up to 62 percent.

To maximize your retention, the following method of study is given. On the first day, read your lesson for Monday and fill in Monday's blanks. On Tuesday, review Monday's questions before reading Tuesday's lesson and filling in Tuesday's blanks. On Wednesday, review the previous two days' questions before reading and filling in the blanks for Wednesday. Continue and do all lessons.

Each week when the *Role Model* comes to check your lesson, he will read each day's questions, and when he comes to a blank, he will help you fill it in. After checking all the blanks, the *Role Model* will lead a discussion of each day's principle.

When you finish the discussion of the week's exercises, you will have reviewed most of the principles six times, and your retention should increase to 62 percent.

WILL IT BE 6% OR 62%?

FOREWORD

This book wasn't written for everyone. It is written only for those who want to hear Jesus say, **Well done,** at the judgment seat of Christ.

This book wasn't written for the people who only want to be pew sitters – who love to sing, fellowship, hear a message, and then go home while turning their eyes toward their coming work week.

This book was written for people who believe that Jesus could come back at any moment.

This book was written for serious-minded Christians who want to learn how to be better Christians.

This book **does not accept** the traditional view of the Great Commission. This book teaches that the Bible is the church's manual and literally declares that our purpose on this earth is to get the gospel to every creature on this earth.

This book **teaches the belief** that everything on this earth was placed here by the Creator to produce after its kind.

- Cattle after their kind

- Creeping things after their kind

- Young people when they get married produce fruit (children) after their kind, and

- The fruit of the righteous (saved) are to produce spiritual fruit after their kind.

When a person is born again and becomes a child of God, he receives a new vocation. He does not need a call to become a soul-winner, because soul winning is his birthright.

He was designed by God to duplicate himself spiritually as well as physically.

The primary purpose of this book is to re-establish the training program Jesus used in training His first disciples.

Our goal is to secure one hundred pastors and churches to become involved in training people well enough so they can train others.

We do not believe in easy believism, and we are not of those who use dynamic means to excite people. We believe the Bible works if we will learn to work the Bible. Our hope is in God's promise of blessing His Word as His people use His Word. We believe we can see the results as recorded in Acts 6:7 become a reality in our churches once again.

And the word of God increased; and the number of the disciples multiplied in Jerusalem greatly; and a great company of the priests were obedient to the faith. (Acts 6:7)

LESSON ONE

THE GREAT COMMISSION WILL SOLVE THE WORLD'S TWO GREATEST NEEDS

Monday

*We must go so others might live!

*For whosoever shall call upon the name of the Lord shall be saved. How then shall they call on him in whom they have not believed? *and how shall they believe in him of whom they have not heard? And how shall they hear without a preacher?* (Romans 10:13-14)

In the beginning was the Word, and the Word was with God, and the Word was God. The same was in the beginning with God . . . And the Word was made flesh, and dwelt among us. (John 1:1-2, 14)

And he said unto them, Go ye into all the world, and preach the gospel to every creature. (Mark 16:15)

THE WORLD'S TWO GREATEST NEEDS

AN OUT-OF-SPACE INVASION

A person from outer space landed on this hostile planet which had no modern transportation, no modern communication or cell phones. To complicate matters people were all dying and faced endless, hopeless pain that would never end. The over-powering pain would consume them. When they died physically, they would drop into a world of blackness and despair – *the rich man also died, and was buried; And in hell he lift up his eyes, being in torments* (Luke 16:22-23).

This world traveler had the antidote. But in order to deliver the antidote, He had to sacrifice His own life.

It wasn't that He had to just die. *He had to die like those He was attempting to save: take their place, endure their pain, suffer putrid illness, and suffer their shame and hopelessness. *Who his own self bare our sins in his own body on the tree, that we, being dead to sins, should live unto righteousness: by whose stripes ye were healed* (1 Peter 2:24).

*He was willing to sacrifice Himself because if He did not die, they would suffer forever. But He had another problem.

Tuesday

They did not know they were sick and needed more than their own religion to cure them. They had to be personally persuaded to receive this only saving antidote. *But they would resist any help! Many of them would become very hostile! They would be hostile toward their own children, their own flesh and blood. But they will suffer this endless agony in this filthy, awful place of torment. *For I am come to set a man at variance against his father, and the daughter against her mother, and the daughter-in-law against her mother-in-law. And a man's foes shall be they of his own household* (Matthew 10:35-36).

They must be persuaded!

If they do not know

If they are not told

If they are not persuaded

They must be told!

They will suffer forever

Suffer forever

Suffer forever

I am willing to save every last one of them.

*I am willing to die for every last one of them.

But it will be USELESS unless they are personally persuaded to take the antidote.

My antidote is USELESS unless people receive it.

Knowing therefore the terror of the Lord, we persuade men (2 Cor. 5:11).

This curse of sin and death will pass on to their children to all generations.

What do you think His greatest problem was?

What do you think His greatest need is? *His greatest need was (is) HOW TO GET the antidote to the hostile masses.

His problem was how could He get this life-saving message to the dying world?

He needed workers. No, He did not need workers; *He needed TRAINED WORKERS.

How could He train workers? *He would establish a place for the distinct purpose of developing trained workers who would carry the antidote to the hostile masses.

Wednesday

THE PLAN FOR GETTING THE MESSAGE OF JESUS TO THE HOSTILE MASSES

He needed a plan that would get the message to the masses. But how? He had no cars, no planes, no newspaper, no television, and no radios or cell phones. How could He reach every one of them **before they died**? Before they perished?

*His decision: "I will establish a local church to be that training center. It must be primarily a training center. My plan would be to begin recruiting workers through the new birth and then begin to train them immediately."

As He began to train workers, the need became even greater. The problem: there were more people being born than were being trained. What is the answer to the problem?

"*I need MORE workers. No! I need MORE TRAINED WORKERS!

"I need a **method that will keep up with the rapid number of people being born** on this earth. But what method of training will accomplish that?

"The successful method would require every person

who is born into my family to become a trainer (Matthew 28:19-20).

"It would seem like a small thing to ask someone who had just been saved from that eternal fire to help me reach their own family and friends and **save them from perishing in that eternal fire.**"

*But what method would lead to rapid growth and still be simple enough for everyone to learn? The method must be both! It must have the ability to reach rapid growth, and it must be easy enough so everyone could do it.

"How about the method in which I teach and show them how to get people saved from hell (receive the antidote, Jesus) in a safe public place. I will show them how to do it. I will teach them how to do it. Then take each one of them out, showing and explaining what and how to win people by giving them on-the-job training until they are developed enough to become a trainer. *And how I kept back nothing that was profitable unto you, but have shewed you, and have taught you publicly, and from house to house* (Acts 20:20).

"When they are trained well enough, I will have two training teams.

"When the two training teams each had trained some-one well enough to train others, we would have four training teams. The four training teams would soon become eight training teams.

"But some of the people will become involved in things of the world and serve themselves instead of serving me. Some will be rebellious and refuse to be trained well enough and will soon quit."

*The answer; "I will call evangelists, pastors, and teachers to motivate and train them – *and some, pastors and teachers; For the perfecting* [developing] *of the saints, for the work of the ministry* (Eph. 4:11-12).

"But what if the evangelists, pastors, and teachers are so busy or lazy or involved in other things in the church that they fail to train others well enough to train others?

"Then many of the masses will die and suffer eternally.

*"I must find evangelists and pastors who love me enough to see that their people are trained well enough to train others.

"I must find people who love me enough to be trained well enough to train others."

Thursday

THE DEVIL'S FULL TIME JOB IS TO STOP THE TRAINING!

The Devil did not understand how to stop Jesus from purchasing our salvation, although he tried. *The Devil's alternate plan was to stop God's marvelous plan of training disciples, training that would soon lead to multiplication, which would reach the masses.

*It took him 200 years to stop the training aspect of soul winning. The method he used was three-fold.

***FIRST**, divide the church into two parts of believers, the laity (members) and the clergy (preachers), and then make witnessing the exclusive job of the clergy.

***SECOND**, magnify the task of reaching every creature on earth so that it becomes so massive that most of the clergy would become discouraged and quit going themselves.

***THIRD**, work to blind people's minds to their personal responsibility in witnessing by blinding their minds to God's magnificent plan so it would never be activated again.

But, there are two things that the Devil could not do concerning God's plan to train workers.

Friday

*FIRST, he could not blot out the simple plan of reaching men with the gospel from God's Word; it is still there. Neither could he stop God from striving with men to be obedient.

SECOND, the Devil could not stop God's people from accepting God's grace and becoming part of the marvelous, simple plan that God charges each one of His children to become involved in.

After Jesus had died and gone back to heaven, angels met the triumphant Saviour. After much praise, imagine one angel approaching Jesus and asking, "Lord, your training plan that trains disciples is marvelous. *It is simple enough for every one of your children to learn and do. But Lord, what if they do not?"

A cloud passed over the face of Jesus as He interrupted the angel. *He said, "They must train! I have no other plan that could reach the masses. THEY MUST TRAIN."

*Now, Jesus asks each evangelist and pastor, "Do you love me enough to train my people?"

Now, Jesus asks each member, "Do you love me enough to duplicate yourself in becoming a trainer?"

*Jesus asks each one of us, "Do you love me ENOUGH?"

MONDAY

1. We must _____ ... so others might
_____ _____!

2. *And how shall they _____ in him of whom they have not _____?*

3. *And he said unto them, _____ _____ _____ _____ _____ _____ and preach the gospel to every creature.* (Mark 16:15)

4. He had to _____ like those He was _____ to save.

5. He was willing to _____ Himself because if He did not die they would _____ forever.

TUESDAY

1. But they would _____ any _____!

2. I am _____ to die for every _____ one of them.

3. His greatest need was (is) _____ _____ _____ the antidote to the hostile masses.

4. He _____ TRAINED _____.

5. He would establish a place for the _____ purpose of _____ trained workers who would carry the antidote to the hostile masses.

WEDNESDAY

1. His decision, I will _____ a local church to be that _____ center.

2. I need more workers. _____! I need MORE _____ WORKERS!

3. But what _____ will lead to _____ growth and still be _____ enough for everyone to learn?

4. The answer; I will call _____, pastors, and teachers to _____ and train them.

5. I must find evangelists and pastors who love me enough to see that their _____ are _____ well enough to _____ others.

THURSDAY

1. The _____ alternate plan was to _____ God's marvelous plan of training disciples.

2. It took him _____ years to stop the training aspect of _____ _____.

3. **FIRST,** _____ the church into two parts of _____;

4. **SECOND,** _____ the task of reaching every creature on earth so that it becomes so _____ that most of the clergy would become _____ and stop going themselves.

5. **THIRD,** work to _____ people's minds to their _____ respon- sibility in _____ by blinding the minds to God's magnificent plan SO IT WOULD _____ BE ACTIVATED AGAIN.

FRIDAY

1. **FIRST**, he could not _____ out the simple plan from reaching men with the _____ from God's Word; it is still there. Neither could he stop God from _____ with men to be obedient.

2. It is _____ enough for every one of your _____ to learn and do.

3. He said, "They_____ _____!

4. Now, Jesus asks each evangelist and _____, "Do you _____ me enough to _____ my people?"

5. Jesus asks each one of _____, "Do you love me..._____?"

DAILY DECLARATION

LESSON ONE

Repeat Aloud Each Morning and Evening

I will strive to be part of extending the Great Commission to every person in the world.

MEMORY VERSE:

And he said unto them, Go ye into all the world, and preach the gospel to every creature. (Mark 16:15)

CHECK BLOCK AFTER REPEATING

	Mon	Tues	Wed	Thurs	Fri	Sat	Sun
A.M.							
P.M.							

After studying this lesion, I will work at doing my part in God's worldwide mission plan of reaching the lost.

_____

Name   **Grade**

LESSON TWO

YOUR NEW VOCATION UNDER THE GREAT COMMISSION

Monday

Have you ever heard the statement, *"Everybody's business is nobody's business"? That pretty well describes what is happening in our twenty-first-century churches concerning the Great Commission.

Do you think that the great, wise God of heaven would be the author of what is going on in many of our churches today? Today, upon his conversion, a person *is all but left to himself to figure out what he should do. Since he has not been taught how to read and rightly divide the Bible, he resorts to learning solely upon observing what other members (Christians) are doing. The old saying, "The blind leading the blind," comes to mind. *Many church members have developed bad habits in their attendance, are unfaithful, and soon become carnal. Since the young convert has no one to develop him in his new vocation, *he begins to follow the bad examples of some church members. *In doing so, he will soon fall back into the world.

THE EPHESIAN'S OLD VOCATION

Tuesday

In the opening verses of chapter two of his letter to the Ephesians, Paul reminded them of their earlier vocation or lifestyle. He told them they were dead or separated from God by their sin. *He said they were living in the world's system and were following the type of life the Devil wanted them to live. *He said their lifestyle (conversation) was spent in pursuing their own selfish desires and interests. They were under the curse of sin and would soon suffer the wrath of God. But in His great love, God sent apostle Paul to preach to them, and they were wonderfully changed. Please read God's description of their old lifestyle and vocation. They were living only for themselves. *And you hath he quickened, who were dead in trespasses and sins; Wherein in time past ye walked according to the course of this world, according to the prince of the power of the air, the spirit that now worketh in the children of disobedience: Among whom also we all had our conversation in times past in the lusts of our flesh, fulfilling the desires of the flesh and of the mind; and were by nature the children of wrath, even as others* (Ephesians 2:1-3).

Later in Ephesians 2:8-10 Paul tells them how they were saved. It was totally by God's wonderful grace. They were not saved by their good works or any righteous deeds they had done. They were offered forgiveness of their sins through the sacrificial death of Jesus on the cross as a free gift. *They were not saved by their good works, **but they were saved to do good works** (to work for and under the Great Commission). Please read verse ten as follows: *For we are his workmanship, created in Christ Jesus unto good works, which God hath before ordained that we should walk in them* (Eph. 2:10).

YOU ARE A SOLDIER IN THE LORD'S ARMY

Although the Bible teaches that you are a soldier in the Lord's army, few accept that fact or view themselves in that light. Paul clearly commands us in Ephesians 6:11 to *Put on the whole armour of God, that ye may be able to stand against the wiles of the devil.*

*One of the wiles or methods of the Devil is to keep us neutral in the war to save people from hell. How does he keep us neutral in the life and death struggle of preventing sinners from going to hell? He works to keep us content to merely attend church and enjoy the fellowship with the saints. *He works to blind our minds to our personal responsibility under the Great Commission. He works to intimidate and make us fearful toward our new vocation. In fact, we are very mindful of how our old vocation did not satisfy our innermost needs, but we are not clear on what our job is as a Christian.

Consider the parallels between a soldier in the United States Army and a soldier in the Lord's army. Does a soldier in the United States Army need training before he goes into combat? If he didn't have proper training before entering into combat, he would very likely become a casualty. At best he would be tentative, fearful, and likely to fail in combat. The same is true concerning you in the Lord's army. That is the reason for your instruction in Ephesians 6:11-19 to put on the *whole armour of God*. This is a very serious matter. Some of your family and friends will suffer if you do not submit to the Lord's will.

In our lesson today we will introduce our new vocation, which we were saved to do or walk after.

THE CHRISTIAN'S NEW VOCATION UNDER THE GREAT COMMISSION

Wednesday

Paul takes almost an entire chapter to explain the Christian's job or vocation: *I THEREFORE, the prisoner of the Lord, beseech you that ye walk worthy of the vocation wherewith ye are called* (Eph. 4:1, emphasis added).

God is so thorough in defining the Christian's job that he states *vocation* and then adds, *wherewith ye are called* in the same sentence. The primary meaning of the word *vocation*, as given in Webster's dictionary, is: "A call or impulsion; to enter a certain career, a career which he believes he is called; any trade, profession or occupation."

Note the double stating of one's vocation in the verse: *Vocation* (a call or impulsion), then adding the definition once again – *werewith ye are called*. God is trying to get across to a newly- saved person that he was called by God to do a certain job.

This definition is in perfect harmony with God's call to four of His new converts in Matthew 4:19 where He said, *Follow me* [in your vocation] *and I will make you fishers of men*. He changed the job or vocation of those men who were commercial fishermen to becoming fishers of men (winning souls).

Paul defines the attitude that each new convert should have in verses two and three of Ephesians 4. He said, *with all lowliness and meekness, with longsuffering, forbearing one another in love; Endeavouring to keep the unity of the Spirit in the bond of peace.*

God gives every member special grace. *The way the word *grace* is defined is as **enabling** grace. This enabling grace **is measured out according to each person's faith**. *But unto every one of us is given grace according to the measure of the gift of Christ* (Ephesians 4:7).

One should always pay special attention to a verse that starts with the words *Wherefore* or *Therefore*. A good rule to follow in Bible interpretation is when a verse starts with the words *Wherefore* or *Therefore*, then one should stop and see what it is **there for**.

Verse one starts with the word *Therefore*, which refers back to the previous verses in Ephesians chapter three. Verse twenty declares the unlimited power of God, which God desires to measure out to all of His children: *Now unto him that is able to do exceeding abundantly above all that we ask or think, according to the power that worketh in us* (Eph. 3:20).

*It is God's power **which worketh in** us or in His children. God is saying that in your new vocation He will supply any power or ability that you need. But He measures it out according to one's faith. If the person draws back in unbelief, God will not be able to help him. If the person believes God and obeys by faith, then God is able to transform him.

In other words, God is saying that it is not your ability that will enable you to win souls and be successful as a Christian doing your new job or vocation. It is Him working through you. So all He requires in order for Him to give you the enabling grace to win souls is for you to trust Him to help you. His enabling grace transformed a sheep herder, Moses, into one of the world's greatest leaders. His enabling grace empowered a convict to be able to save the nation of Israel. His enabling grace will change the lowly apostles into prominent kings during the 1000-year reign. His enabling grace was able to take a backslidden and carnal man, Samson, and use him mightily. His enabling grace is especially powerful to the poor, the base, and the average person. *By His grace you can become one of His best soul-winners.

GOD GAVE SPECIAL ABILITY TO EVANGELISTS, PASTORS, AND TEACHERS

Thursday

Not only will God work in you to enable you, but He will call special men into the ministry to help to train you.

And he gave some, apostles; and some, prophets; and some, evangelists; and some, pastors and teachers. (Ephesians 4:11)

There were five different gifts given to these special trainers or equippers. The office worker type of apostles and prophets have fulfilled their purpose and are no longer in effect. Now God calls evangelists, pastors, and teachers into full-time ministry. Verse twelve reveals why these men are called: *it is to perfect the saints so they can do the work of the ministry. The word *perfect* means to become highly skilled in doing the things which will fulfill the Great Commission.

When one obeys the Bible and learns to do the work

of the ministry, he experiences spiritual growth and becomes a mature Christian who will joyfully and faithfully serve God.

WALKING WORTHY OF ONE'S VOCATION

Paul begs the new converts in the Ephesian church to walk worthy of their new vocation in obeying the Great Commission.

*The primary emphasis in obeying the Great Commission is preaching or telling the gospel to every person. In order for a person to be able to win souls, there must be three things in his life:

First, he must put off his former lifestyle. In his effort to entice the new converts in winning their family and friends, Paul told them in verse 22 to change their life-style. *That ye put off concerning the former conversation the old man, which is corrupt according to the deceitful lusts* (Eph. 4:22). In this verse Paul is instructing them to change the way they were living: to stop following the fleshly desires and begin learning a new lifestyle as a Christian.

Second, he tells them how to put off their former life-style. In verse 23 Paul says they can do it by renewing their minds by studying and obeying the Bible to *be renewed in the spirit of your mind.*

Third, he instructs them to put on their new vocation.
This instruction is given in verse 24 where he states,
And that ye put on the new man – in other words, *leave
your old way of life for a new, exciting one by learning
your new vocation.

Peter told his new converts in 2 Peter 1:5-7 to add to
their faith (saving faith) virtue or good habits. Then
add to virtue knowledge. To gain knowledge one is to
continue adding Christian characteristics by DOING
THEM. Those characteristics are listed as temperance,
patience, godliness, brotherly kindness, and godly love
(charity).

The author is attempting to show that *being a Christian
is not just believing doctrine and being moral. It is his
new vocation or job, and he is not only learning how to
do the job, but he is to walk (do) worthy of being one
of Jesus' disciples.

WHY IS THE UNDERSTANDING
OF THE CHRISTIAN LIFE AS A
VOCATION IMPORTANT?

The reasons it is important to understand that being a
Christian is a new vocation are as follows:

First, *it identifies that a person was saved for a particular job or reason. He was not saved just to learn about

the Christian life and doctrine. He was saved to learn how to do his new vocation or job.

Second, if being a Christian is a vocation, he can learn how to do his job well. People learn what their vocation is, and then someone demonstrates how to do the job. After they are shown, they begin to do the job while under supervision. After they are given on-the-job experience, they are able to be skilled in their new vocation.

FRIDAY

Third, the way a person learns how to do any job is to know the method of doing the job. *Someone explains what the job is and how to do it. Then, the new trainee (Christian) is shown how to do the job in a classroom or home (Acts 5:42). *The new Christian's job is to learn how to win his family, friends, and others. After the trainee (Christian) is shown how to do his new vocation of winning souls, he must receive some on-the-job training. This is where the evangelist, pastor, or teacher comes in. His specific job is to work with the new convert by going with him to his lost friends, family, or others and showing him how to win them by winning them.

*This vocational training of showing and doing is to continue until the new convert is good at giving the plan of salvation and winning others to Christ. The trainee's job or vocation then takes on a new dimension.

*He becomes the trainer who helps others in learning their new vocation of winning and discipling others.

PRACTICE MAKES PERFECT

*The old saying "Practice makes perfect" is very true in learning to give the plan of salvation and win souls. At first the believer delivers the four spiritual principles in an awkward manner. But just like learning to play the piano, the more the new musician practices, the more confidence he acquires. The more confidence he acquires, the better he is at giving the plan of salvation. The same principle is true in learning to be a good ball player. When young athletes first start playing ball, they are awkward and uncoordinated. But the more they practice the better they are able to play. It is similarly true in learning the new vocation of soul winning. The more you practice, the better you will be able to witness to and win souls. Jesus promised that if you follow Him, He will teach you to do your new job of winning souls.

MONDAY

1. "Everybody's _____ is
_____ business?"

2. Is all but _____ to himself to _____
out what he should do.

3. Many church members have _____
bad habits in their _____ and are
unfaithful.

4. He begins to _____ the bad
_____ of some church members;

5. In doing so he will _____ _____
back into the world.

TUESDAY

1. He said they were living in the _____
system and were _____ the type of
life the _____ wanted them to live.

2. He said their lifestyle (_____)
was spent in _____ their own
selfish desires and interests.

3. They were not saved _____ their good works, but
they were saved _____ _____ good works.

4. One of the wiles or _____ of
the Devil is to keep us _____ in
the war to save people from hell.

5. He works to _____ our minds
to our _____ responsibility under
the Great Commission.

WEDNESDAY

1. Vocation (a _____ or impulsion), then adding the _____ once
again – *Wherewith ye are called.*

2. *Follow me* [in your _____] *and
I will make you* _____ *of men.*

3. The way the word *grace* is defined is as

_____ _____.

4. It is God's _____ which
_____ in us or in His children.

5. By His _____ you can become one of
His _____ soul-winners.

THURSDAY

1. It is to _____ the saints so they can
do the _____ of the ministry.

2. The primary _____ in obeying
the Great Commission is _____ or
_____ the gospel.

3. Leave your _____ _____ of life for a
new, exciting one by _____ your
new vocation.

4. Being a Christian is not just _____
doctrine and being _____.

5. It identifies that a person was _____
for a particular _____ or reason.

FRIDAY

1. Someone _____ what the
_____ _____ and how to do it.

2. The new Christian's _____ is to learn
how to win his _____, friends,
and _____.

3. This vocational training of _____
and _____ is to continue until
the new convert is _____ at giving the
plan of salvation.

4. He becomes the _____ who
helps _____ in learning their
new vocation.

5. The old saying "_____ makes
_____" is very true in learning
to _____ the plan of salvation.

DAILY DECLARATION

Lesson Two

Repeat Aloud Each Morning and Evening

I accept my new life vocation and will strive to be obedient to the Lord.

MEMORY VERSE:

The fruit of the righteous is a tree of life; and he that winneth souls is wise (Proverbs 11:30).

CHECK BLOCK AFTER REPEATING

	Mon	Tues	Wed	Thurs	Fri	Sat	Sun
A.M.							
P.M.							

I will work at learning God's powerful four spiritual principles and will strive to tell people about God's love.

Name   **Grade**

LESSON THREE

WHAT DID JESUS MEAN WHEN HE GAVE THE GREAT COMMISSION?

In Mark 16:14-15 Jesus said:

> *Afterward he appeared unto the eleven as they sat at meat, and upbraided them with their unbelief and hardness of heart because they believed not them which had seen him after he was risen. And he said unto them, Go ye into all the world, and preach the gospel to every creature.*

Monday

There is no doubt as to what He said. I think if you had been in that room you would have never forgotten what He said. He didn't have the whip that He used to run the money changers out of the temple. But His countenance and spirit were the same as when *He gave those in that room a tongue lashing due to their unbelief and hardness of heart.

Do you think that Jesus got their attention?

Your answer would be yes; *those in the room would be totally focused on Jesus and what He was saying.

After Jesus had gotten their full attention, *He spoke

those immortal words that this generation does not understand!

He said, *Go into all the world and preach the gospel to every creature.*

In order for our generation to understand this verse, let us turn to the laws of proper Bible interpretation.

1. Who is speaking? Jesus

2. To whom is He speaking? *To His leaders of the one local church that had at least 120 dedicated members, including the twelve apostles (Acts 1:15).

3. What was He talking about? He was telling His one local church that had a small membership to:

- Go into all the world

- To preach, publish, tell, or proclaim the gospel

- The gospel, or the good news, is that there is a God who loves them and has paid for their sins by giving His Son to die for every man, woman, boy, and girl's sins.

4. When was this command given? This command was given right after Jesus had proven He was God by taking up His life on the third day (Romans 1:4).

WHAT DID JESUS MEAN?

Tuesday

It is clear what Jesus said in Mark 16:14-15, but what did He mean?

*Did He mean that they were to set up a mission program so they could fulfill the Great Commission by giving to missionaries in the remote areas of the earth?

Did He really mean that those who made up the membership of *that one, small local church were to literally get the good story of love and forgiveness of God to every creature that lived upon the earth?

*Was Jesus speaking prophetically or literally? Was He speaking about some far-off time in 2014? *Was He giving this generation some plan for worldwide missions, or did He literally expect the members of one, small local church to get the gospel to every person on the earth?

HOW DID THE MEMBERS OF THE ONE LOCAL CHURCH UNDERSTAND HIS ABSOLUTE COMMAND?

This command was given around 200 years ago to people just like you and me who made up the first local church. *How did those first members react to Jesus' command to get the good news of God's love and forgiveness to every person alive on planet earth?

Wednesday

WHAT DID MEMBERS OF THE FIRST CHURCH BELIEVE?

*They believed that Jesus meant what He said. They were to get the wonderful news of God's marvelous plan of redemption to every person on earth.

How do we know they believed that Jesus literally meant for them to get the gospel to every creature on earth?

*We know what they believed by what they did. Their obedience to Jesus' command is recorded in the pages of God's inspired record.

- They were told to wait for the filling and empowering Spirit of God (Luke 24:49).

- *On the day of Pentecost they won and baptized 3000 people.

- *Through praising the Lord and witnessing, they had daily additions to the church (Acts 2:46). If there were people added to your church on a daily basis for five years, and this daily addition added up to an average of 600 per year, then over a five-year period there would be another 3000 people added to the church. We have 3000 (on the day of Pentecost) and 3000 (daily additions), or 6000 additions.

- *Upon the healing of the lame man and the witnessing and preaching of the apostles, they had another 5000 men get saved (Acts 4:4). So, there were 3000 on the day of Pentecost, another 3000 in the daily additions, and now 5000, for an approximate total of 11,000 people saved.

Thursday

*This marvelous winning of souls was next described in Acts 5:14 as *multitudes*. Please note the word *multitudes* is plural, which means more than one multitude. It could have been many multitudes. We don't know how many multitudes there were or how many people were in the multitudes, but for the sake of numbers, let's say there were two multitudes. Jesus fed two multitudes during His personal ministry. Let us take the number in the two multitudes of 4000 and 5000 men who were fed in order to illustrate the marvelous growth that the one local church that took Jesus literally was having. We had 3000 on the day of Pentecost, we estimated that the number added to the church over a period of five years to be another 3000. Five thousand men were saved on one day and now if we estimate 4000 in one multitude and another 5000 men in the other multitude, these great results add up to a total of 20,000 people saved.

*The reader may wonder, "Why this attempt to establish the possible number of people being saved?"

*__First__, it is evident the members of the first church took Jesus' command to get the good news of God's love to every creature seriously.

*__Second__, we want to establish the success of God's plan. One cannot get an idea of the success of God's plan by saying, "daily additions or multitudes were being saved," but he can estimate the numbers in the daily additions and in the multitudes being saved and give them a total, just as we did.

Why would we do this? *In order to give a clear picture of the working of God's great plan to get the gospel to every person on the earth.

Friday

* Acts 6:1 records the following statement: __The number of the disciples was MULTIPLIED.__ One cannot multiply "daily additions" or "multitudes," but he can multiply the figure of 20,000. Multiply 20,000 by 2 and you have the startling figure of 40,000 additions to the one local church in about five years.

God never told the members of the first church to build

a church on the north side of town and minister to their members. But He did say, "Get the gospel to every creature in all the world."

In Acts 6:7 we have another reference to the success of the first church that took literally Jesus' command to get the gospel to every creature in the whole world. Notice how exact this statement of the success of the first church (in Jerusalem) was: *And the word of God increased.*

Everything they did was based not upon a traditional understanding of God's Word, but upon the literal obedience to God's Word. *Note the results of their obedience: *and the number of the disciples multiplied in Jerusalem greatly; and a great company of the priests were obedient to the faith* (Acts 6:7).

Multiply 40,000 perhaps by the number five or ten, and what do you have? You have enough citizens in the city of Jerusalem saved and baptized to cause the leaders of the city and the Jewish religion to protest! *Their words were *ye have filled Jerusalem with your doctrine.* (Acts 5:28b).

Now, the one church in Jerusalem is giving birth to other churches in Judea, Galilee, and Samaria. GUESS WHAT? *These churches in Judea, Galilee, and Samaria are multiplying by winning and training souls as well (Acts 9:31).

***SUMMARY**: The first local church literally believed they were to get the story of God's love and forgiveness to every creature. They proved it by their action.

The first church that started with just a few members was able to win and train enough workers that they evangelized the whole world. But how did they do it? Could it be done in our day?

We will answer these questions in our next lesson.

MONDAY

1. He _____ those in that room a tongue
_____.

2. Those in the room would be totally
_____ on Jesus and what He was
_____.

3. He spoke those _____ words
which this generation _____ _____ understand!

4. *Go into all the _____ and preach the
gospel to _____ creature.*

5. To His _____ of the one local church
that had at least 120 _____ members

TUESDAY

1. Did He mean that they were to set up a
_____ _____?

2. That one, small local church were to
_____ get the good story of love
and _____ of God to every
creature.

3. Was Jesus speaking _____ or
_____?

4. Was He giving this generation some _____ for _____ missions?

5. How did those _____ members react to Jesus' _____?

WEDNESDAY

1. They _____ that _____ meant what He said.

2. We _____ what they believed by what they _____.

3. On the day of _____ they won and _____ 3000 people.

4. Through praising the Lord and _____, they had _____ additions to the church (Acts 2:46).

5. Upon the healing of the lame man and the witnessing and _____ of the _____ they had another _____ men get saved (Acts 4:4).

THURSDAY

1. This marvelous _____ of souls was next described in Acts 5:14 as _____.

2. The reader may wonder, "Why this _____ to establish the possible _____ of people being saved?"

3. **First**, it is evident the _____ of the first church took Jesus' _____ to get the good news of _____ love to every creature seriously.

4. **Second**, we want to _____ the _____ of God's _____.

5. In order to give a clear _____ of the working of God's _____ plan to get the gospel to _____ person on the earth.

FRIDAY

1. Acts 6:1 records the following statement, *the
_____ of the disciples was

_____.*

2. Note the results of their _____:
*and the _____ of disciples multi-
plied in Jerusalem _____*

3. Their words were, *ye have _____
Jerusalem with your _____.*

4. These churches in _____,
_____, and
_____ are multiplying in winning and _____ souls as well
(Acts 9:31).

5. **SUMMARY**: The _____ _____
church literally believed they were to get the story of
God's love and _____ to every
creature.

DAILY DECLARATION

Lesson Three

Repeat Aloud Each Morning and Evening

I will strive to follow the Bible and not man's traditional interpretation of the Great Commission.

MEMORY VERSE:

And he saith unto them, Follow me, and I will make you fishers of men. (Matthew 4:19)

CHECK BLOCK AFTER REPEATING

	Mon	Tues	Wed	Thurs	Fri	Sat	Sun
A.M.							
P.M.							

I will strive to be directed by man's greatest need, which is to keep eternal souls from going to hell.

_____

Name   **Grade**

LESSON FOUR

HOW DID THE FIRST CHURCH OBEY THE GREAT COMMISSION IN DEVELOPING THEIR CONVERTS INTO SOUL WINNERS?

Monday

In our second lesson on Mark 16:14-15, we saw that the members of the first, small local church literally believed that *Jesus meant for them to get the gospel to every creature in the whole world. They not only believed that He meant for them to give every person a chance to escape the horrors of suffering eternally in hell by giving them His message of love and forgiveness, *but the first lesson proves they did it.

In the next two lessons, we will not only explain HOW they developed their converts into soul winners, but *WHO developed them into soul winners AND WHY.

*WHAT DOES THAT REMARKABLE FEAT OF GETTING THE GOSPEL TO THE WHOLE WORLD IN THEIR GENERATION MEAN TO US?

We know they preached the gospel to the whole world in their generation, because the early church fathers and early reformers believed and taught that they did. In addition, the Bible records that fact. *But the question arises, **"How did they do it?"**

Tuesday

We will attempt to answer part of those questions in our lesson today. We will do so by examining what the Great Commission according to Matthew.

> *And Jesus came and spake unto them, saying, All power is given unto me in heaven and in earth. Go ye therefore, and teach all nations, baptizing them in the name of the Father, and of the Son, and of the Holy Ghost: Teaching them to observe all things whatsoever I have commanded you: and, lo, I am with you alway, even unto the end of the world. Amen. (Matthew 28:18-20)*

Before studying the Great Commission as given in Matthew 28:18-20, please consider **what is at stake**.

*Jesus came into the world to save the perishing masses from hell. He proved the sincerity of His love for each person on the earth by dying on the cross as their sub-stitution. **Are these statements true?**

Paul asked these questions in Romans 10:14:

- How can they believe upon Him whom they have not heard?

- *How shall they hear without a preacher (publisher or teller)?

If they hear of His love and provision and accept Him as Saviour, they will receive forgiveness of sin and eternal life. If they do not hear and die in their sins, they will be lost forever. **Is the author still right?**

WHICH IS MORE LOGICAL?

Our God is perfect in wisdom, power, and love. Would He leave it up to frail man to devise a plan, *or would He place His plan within the local church and record it in His eternal Word?

Would He allow frail man to devise a plan which may change from man to man? Or would He place a clear method of training that would never change within His local church and have it be revealed in His eternal Word?

According to Matthew, the Commission literally says: upon my authority go into all the world and disciple the people of all nations. Baptize them in the name (by authority) of the Father, the Son and of the Holy Ghost.

*It is in verse twenty that most Bible teachers are **blinded by traditional interpretation** of the Great Commission. They interpret verse twenty to say, teaching them all things whatsoever I have commanded you. *In doing so they cause the meaning of the Commission according to Matthew **to become completely obscure**. Their interpretation makes the Great Commission according to Matthew say:

- Win souls
- Baptize the converts
- Then teach them "All things of God"

Wednesday

Such a stress on these verses makes Christianity a mere philosophy that people just teach as "The Word." *This interpretation literally guts the Great Commission and makes these verses teach church authority and a basis for preaching Faith Promise Missions. Now, these verses can be used to teach both of these wonderful doctrines, but these verses teach much more!

Before I give the Bible interpretation of the Great Commission according to Matthew, please consider the following:

*Jesus did command **His one local church** *to go*, but this is not grammatically true here in Matthew. He did not use the imperative verb *go* in this verse. He did use an imperative verb in Mark 16:15 when He said, *Go into all the world and preach the gospel to every creature.* But here in Matthew, *go* is not a command. In the original text it is a circumstantial participle which means, "as (or since or while) you are going." It is an aorist participle and literally translated reads, "having gone turning people into disciples."

*It is a very sobering thought to realize that at the end of every day God examines your *having gone* with serious scrutiny to see whether **you have obeyed or disobeyed** the mandate of Jesus to turn people into disciples. *According to Matthew, the spirit and sense in the Great Commission is on observing and doing, not on just teaching the Word. The words and the way Jesus used them indicated excitement and action.

In the latter part of Acts chapter two, *we find the joy and excitement of a successful church training its members in soul winning: *Praising God, and having favour with all the people. And the Lord added to the church daily such as should be saved* (Acts 2:47).

Can you imagine what would happen when the membership was being obedient to the command of "as you go [live] make men into disciples"? Can you visualize the joy of the fulfillment found in Acts 5:42: *And daily in the temple, and in every house, they ceased not to teach and preach Jesus Christ.*

We know you can develop a dedicated church member into an obedient soul winner who has the new joy and excitement, because we have done it.

WHAT DOES THE COMMISSION IN MATTHEW REALLY TEACH?

Thursday

In Matthew 16:18 Jesus told His disciples that *upon this rock* (Jesus), *I will build my church* (1 Corinthians 10:4). He chose Matthew to reveal how He would build His church in Matthew's account of the Great Commission.

Matthew was formerly a tax collector and was used to doing things in a professional way. He had to be exact in all of his dealings, or he would be in danger from the crooked element in the tax collecting business. *In his account of the Great Commission, he gave **the methodology of how Jesus would build His church**. He also gave the duration of the Great Commission, which was *from that present day until the end of the world or age.

THERE ARE FIVE PRINCIPLES TO UNDERSTAND

In order to have a clear understanding of the Commission given in Matthew, there are five principles to understand.

1. The Commission was given to the church. The church was made up of saved, baptized members, not preachers only. When Jesus gave the Commission in Matthew, He was speaking to the individuals who made up the church. *There is no such thing as a mystical institution called the "Church." He gave the Commission **to the people who were the church.**

2. The first responsibility of the church was to win souls. Jesus had already taught them how to win souls. He said, *Follow me and I will make you fishers of men* (Matthew 4:19). *The members had been part of a soul-winning team in training for three-and-a-half years. They knew well what their first responsibility as a Christian was. It was to witness and win souls.

3. They were to train others to win souls. Jesus' statement in Matthew 28:20 teaching them *to observe all things* was made to the same people as in verses 18 and 19. It was to the people or members of that church that this command, *teaching them to observe* [do] *all things,* was given. That statement means that the members were

to learn how to disciple and win souls well enough to train others to disciple and win souls.

4. These commands were made in order for that one local church to be able to go into all the world and teach all nations. *Each member was to be involved in winning and discipling converts. This knowledge and ability was to the extent that they would take others out and train them to win souls.

Friday

5. *The first church was **set up to be a training institution** and not merely an institution to teach doctrines and morals and for fellowship.

THE CHURCH WAS TO TRAIN
EVERY MEMBER

*As stated, the church was responsible for developing its members in soul winning and discipling. The Bible is also very specific about who trains and how the members are to be trained.

WHO IS RESPONSIBLE FOR
DEVELOPING THE MEMBERS?

In Ephesians 4:11-12 the Bible declares that *God called men into the ministry and gave them the responsibility of training the members.

In those verses He states that He called evangelists, pastors, and teachers and **gave them the job of perfecting or training the members** of the church to do the work of the ministry. *The work of the ministry or church is in the areas of prayer, soul winning, and discipling.

The evangelists, pastors, and teachers were to perfect the members. *Perfect means to train to **a high level of ability and performance**.

In the next lesson we will show how the members were developed into soul winners and why.

MONDAY

1. Jesus meant for them to get the gopel
to every _____ in the

_____ _____.

2. But the first lesson _____ they

_____ _____.

3. WHO _____ them into soul
winners AND _____.

4. What does that _____ feat
of getting the gospel to the whole world in their
_____ mean to us?

5. But the _____ arises,
"_____ did they do it?"

TUESDAY

1. Jesus came into the world to save the
_____ masses from

_____.

2. How shall they _____ without a _____, (publisher or
_____)?

3. Or would He _____ His
plan within the _____
_____ and record it in His eternal Word?

4. It is in verse twenty that most Bible teachers are _____ by _____ interpretation of the Great Commission.

5. In doing so they cause the _____ of the Commission according to _____ to become completely _____.

WEDNESDAY

1. This interpretation _____ guts the _____ Commission.

2. Jesus did command His one _____ church *to go*, but this is not _____ true here in Matthew.

3. It is a very _____ thought to realize that at the end of every day God _____ your having gone.

4. The spirit and sense in the Great Commission according to Matthew is on _____ and _____.

5. We find the _____ and _____ of a successful church training its members in _____ _____.

THURSDAY

1. In his account of the Great Commission he gave the _____ of how Jesus would _____ His church.

2. From that _____ day until the _____ of the world or age.

3. There is no such thing as a _____ institution called the "_____."

4. The members had been part of a soul winning _____ in training for _____ years.

5. _____ member was to be involved in winning and _____ converts.

FRIDAY

1. The first church was set up to be a

_____ _____.

2. As stated, the church was _____

for _____ its members in soul

winning and discipling.

3. God _____ men into

the ministry and gave them the responsibility of

_____ the members.

4. The work of the ministry or church is in the areas of

_____, _____ _____,

and _____.

5. _____ means to train to a

high _____ of ability and

_____.

DAILY DECLARATION

Lesson Four

Repeat Aloud Each Morning and Evening

I will submit to learning how to win souls by becoming a silent partner trainee.

MEMORY VERSE:

I am debtor both to the Greeks, and to the Barbarians; both to the wise, and to the unwise. (Romans 1:14)

CHECK BLOCK AFTER REPEATING

	Mon	Tues	Wed	Thurs	Fri	Sat	Sun
A.M.							
P.M.							

Since God commanded the pastors to perfect me so I can be very good at winning souls, I will practice giving the plan of salvation every day.

Name   **Grade**

LESSON FIVE

HOW AND WHY DID THE PREACHERS PERFECT THE SAINTS?

Monday

In this lesson we will present from the Scriptures the method and the motivation that the preachers used to raise a mighty army that evangelized their world.

First, how did they do it? They followed the method of the One who was an example to His followers. Acts 1:1 states that Jesus began to DO and to teach. *The doing meant He practiced what He taught. The doing, or example, came before the teaching.

Second, in this important task of training or perfecting the saints, the pastors were examples. 1 Peter 5:3 states, *but being examples to the flock*. The pastors were over the local flock or church (Acts 20:28), *and as such they were to teach their members by word and example.

*Third, the membership was to submit to the pastor's example, leadership, and training**. Hebrews 13:7 commands the members *whose faith follow, considering the end of their conversation* [life]. Hebrews 13:17 says, *Obey them that have the rule over you, and submit yourselves.*

*How can the preachers bring their members to a high level of performance in soul winning?

*The literal interpretation of the Bible is that Christians are to learn how to win souls so they can develop or train others to win souls.

It is also clear that God called preachers to train or perfect their members to win souls.

The word *perfect* means to develop them in soul winning, until they are good soul winners who will be able to teach others.

The question arises, "How can this command be obeyed?"

Tuesday

BEING A CHRISTIAN IS A VOCATION

In Ephesians 4:1 Paul begs the members of the church at Ephesus, *I therefore, the prisoner of the Lord, beseech you that ye walk worthy of the vocation wherewith ye are called.* *When one is saved, he has a new vocation, which is to represent Jesus and bring His message to a lost world.

In answering this question **one must remember that being a Christian is a vocation**. Once a person accepts that being a soul winner or Christian is a vocation, it is easy to answer this question of how a person could be developed to a high level of ability and performance in soul winning.

*In any vocation a trainee is **first instructed on how to do the work**. *After they are told how to do it, then **they are shown how to do it**. A journeyman or trainer would first do the work, showing and explaining the procedure. Then, he would be a watchful coach as the new trainee began to perform the operation.

This is exactly how the leaders in the first church perfected their members to do **the vocation of winning souls** (Acts 5:42). They explained and demonstrated the principles of soul winning in a classroom or home. *They walked through the steps as they explained what they were doing. Then they would take the new convert or trainee out and show and teach them as they were winning souls.

One may inquire, "Is there a verse which explains that procedure of training?"

The answer is, "Yes." *And daily in the temple, and in every house, they ceased not to teach and preach Jesus Christ* (Acts 5:42).

This verse states when the training took place: there was training going on every day.

This verse states where this training was being given: there was daily on-the-job training going on in the temple area (publicly), as well as daily training going on in different houses.

Notice who was doing the training: It was "they," meaning *there were laymen doing the training as well as preachers.

Note what type of training was going on: It was from house to house as well as in a public place.

Wednesday

*The word *teach* means to disciple or train new believers. The word *preach* means to proclaim Christ as Saviour or "to win souls." The main business of the church was to teach (train) or develop their members by giving them lessons in the home as well as in the public services. They were to do so for those new members who **accepted their new vocation of being a Christian**. This was done in public as they were taken out and given on-the-job training as they went into the homes of their city.

One may inquire, "Is there another verse which explains that type of vocational training?"

The answer is, "Yes."

PAUL SHOWED AND TAUGHT HIS CONVERTS

Please note this procedure in Acts 20:20:

And how I kept back nothing that was profitable unto you, but have shewed you, and have taught you publicly, and from house to house.

*First, he taught the people by being a good example. Note the statement, *how I kept back nothing that was profitable unto you*, means he was a good example. In Acts 20:31 he said he was a good example to them for three years.

Second, *but have shewed you, and have taught you publicly*: *He walked through the procedure of winning a soul in a classroom. *He demonstrated how to do each thing as he explained it.

Third, after showing and teaching them how to win souls in a classroom, *he would take them out and give them on-the-job training**. He would continue this training until the person learned well enough to win souls. Then **he would lend a watchful eye** as the new trainee developed to a level where he began training another trainee.

Thursday

WHY DID THE PASTORS WORK SO HARD IN TRAINING THEIR MEMBERS?

The reason the pastors gave themselves to the training of the Word in a public classroom followed by giving their members on-the-job training from house to house is that *it is **the only way a person can be trained to be good in any vocation**, especially the vocation of soul winning. After the tremendous growth that the church in Jerusalem experienced, the pastors had a hard time doing their primary work of perfecting (training) the many new members. They begged the church to relieve them of some of their lesser duties. This was because they wanted to give themselves to prayer and the ministry of the Word (Acts 6:4).

*This "ministry of the Word" did not mean going to their library and studying the Word. It meant the very opposite. It meant that they could conduct the training classes and fully develop the new members in their new vocation of winning souls. That aspect of the ministry of the Word *was borne out while they were giving on-the-job training in the community.

Apostle Paul explained how he trained his members and WHY in 1 Thessalonians 2:7-12.

In verse seven he stated that he treated the new converts as gently as a nurse cares for a newborn baby.

In verse eight he stated that his new spiritual children were so dear to him that he would lay down his life for them.

In verse nine he reminds them how hard he worked to win and train them. It was day and night.

In verse ten he reminded them of how holy and justly and blamelessly he behaved himself as he was training them. The choice of the word *behavior* gives an important insight into training new converts who were learning their new vocation of being a Christian. How can a domestic baby learn to be an obedient member of the family? Since he cannot read or write, he learns proper behavior by observing his older brothers and sisters. The greatest teacher of a child is his mother and father's behavior and role modeling. So it is with our spiritual babies; *they learn by observing the behavior of the pastor as well as listening to what he teaches.

In verse eleven he states as a father how he exhorted, comforted, and charged the disciples as he gave them their training. *It was the same method as that of a father who is training his children.

Friday

Verse twelve answers the question of why he worked so hard in training them. It reveals why he lived as their role model and as a father to bring up good, obedient Christians who could perform their new vocation. Note the verse: *that ye would walk worthy of God, who hath called you unto his kingdom and glory.*

Why did Paul give such gentle training to new babies in Christ? His answer is *that they would walk worthy of God in their new vocation as children of God.*

Why did Paul work so hard in developing new disciples? It was so they could occupy an honorable position in the coming millennial kingdom, where they would rule and reign with Christ for 1000 years.

Why did Paul labor night and day, first as a gentle nurse and then as a loving spiritual father? It was because he knew that what they did as a Christian on this earth would not only give them an honored reward in the millennium, but would give them a greater opportunity to hear Jesus say, *Well done thou good and faithful servant: enter into sharing My eternal glory* (Matthew 25:21).

But the main thing Paul knew was that the tough training would be used of God to save thousands of people from going to hell.

STUDY THESE FINAL WORDS OF ENCOURAGEMENT

*First, **anyone could learn to win souls** if they were shown and taught how in a classroom, and this tutoring was followed by being a silent partner trainee in soul-winning efforts. They would watch, learn, and gain confidence as they were trained by their instructor.

Second, if one used this method of training, it would soon reach the level we have seen in the book of Acts. *And the word of God increased*; it caused the number of disciples to multiply (Acts 6:7).

Third, God placed this marvelous training procedure in a local church in order to get the marvelous message of His love to the complete world.

*__Fourth__, we are still under the Great Commission – *even unto the end of the world* [age] (Matthew 28:20).

*__Fifth__, this means that **we are still under the method to perfect the church membership** so they can win and train their converts to win souls.

*__Finally__, it is clear that **Jesus placed a method of training in His local church** that would soon result in the multiplying of the disciples and a worldwide revival.

This same type of training could bring a revival in America.

Our next lesson will show **how we can overcome our day of apostasy** and have a revival.

MONDAY

1. The _____ meant He _____ what He taught.

2. And as such they were to teach their members by _____ and _____.

3. **Third, the _____ was to submit to the pastor's example, _____,
and training** (Hebrews 13:7).

4. How can the _____ bring their members to a _____ level of performance in soul winning?

5. The literal interpretation of the _____ is that Christians are to _____how to win souls so they can develop or _____ others to win souls.

TUESDAY

1. When one is saved, he has a new _____, which is to _____ Jesus and bring His message to a lost world.

2. In any vocation a _____ is first _____ on how to do the work.

3. After they are told how to _____ it, then they are _____ how to do it.

4. They _____ through the steps as they _____ what they were doing.

5. There were _____ doing the training as well as _____.

WEDNESDAY

1. The word _____ means to _____ or train new believers.

2. First, he _____ the people by being a good _____.

3. He walked through the _____ of winning a soul in a _____.

4. He _____ how to do each thing as he _____ it.

5. He would take them out and give them _____-_____-_____ training.

THURSDAY

1. It is the _____ way a person can be trained
to be _____ in any vocation.

2. This ministry of the Word did not mean
going to their _____ and
_____ the Word.

3. Was _____ out while they
were _____ on-the-job training in the
_____.

4. They learn by _____ the
behavior of the pastor as well as listening to what he
_____.

5. It was the same method as that of a
_____ who is training his
_____.

FRIDAY

1. First, _____ could _____
to win souls.

2. *And the Word of God increased*; it
_____ the number of disciples to
_____ (Acts 6:7).

3. Fourth, we are _____ under the Great
Commission – *even unto the end of the* _____
[age]... (Acts 28:20).

4. Fifth, this means that we are still under the
_____ to _____ the
church membership so they can train their converts
to win souls.

5. Finally, it is _____ that Jesus
placed a method of training in His local church that would
soon _____ in the multiplying.

DAILY DECLARATION

Lesson Five

Repeat Aloud Each Morning and Evening

I will strive to become a trainer in our church's soul-winning training program.

MEMORY VERSE:

And the things that thou hast heard of me among many witnesses, the same commit thou to faithful men, who shall be able to teach others also. (2 Timothy 2:2)

CHECK BLOCK AFTER REPEATING

	Mon	Tues	Wed	Thurs	Fri	Sat	Sun
A.M.							
P.M.							

I will become a better Christian and soul winner as I submit to the Great Commission, which commands me to train others.

_____

Name   Grade

LESSON SIX

OBEYING THE GREAT COMMISSION WILL BRING NATIONAL REVIVAL

Monday

WE CAN HAVE NATIONAL REVIVAL IN OUR DAY

*The Bible absolutely promises that we can have national revival in America in our day. By national revival, I mean returning America back to a moral, Christian nation. To be even clearer in our definition, I am speaking of a national revival that would return America to what it was like sixty years ago.

*God gave the recipe or simple principles which promise that national revival. We will examine those principles in this lesson and fully explain them.

First, let me say, if we do not have national revival, the grandchildren of many of the people reading this lesson will spend eternity suffering in the fires of hell. *America is following in the steps of decline as was experienced in the land of England, which now has less that 2 percent of their people in church on any given Sunday. At one time England led the world in sending out missionaries, but now she suffers as a totally pagan nation.

*America is losing 80 percent of its teenagers within two years of graduation from high school. At this rate of loss, coupled with the death of our senior citizens, we will be down to that percentage in a few short years. *Most of this generation's grandchildren will suffer in the fires of hell because of the neglect and apathy of their grandparents.

We will clearly show the steps which will prevent that tragedy and bring national revival later in this lesson.

Tuesday

UNDERSTANDING THE TENDENCY OF MAN

Before the average Christian will believe we can have national revival in our day, he must have faith. *Faith cometh by hearing and hearing by the word of God* (Romans 10:17). *Using the Word of God, we will clearly show the tendency of man to turn back to apostasy.

The wrong concept of apostasy and revival.

Most of this generation of believers has the wrong concept of our day. They believe that America was always a godly, holy nation until this generation, when we slipped into the last days. They believe that the last days is a period right before the second coming of Jesus and that we are powerless to do anything about our apostasy.

They are wrong in their belief on both counts.

*First, they are wrong as to when the last days started. The last days didn't begin in our modern generation. The Bible clearly teaches that the last days started during the ministry of Jesus. *The Bible pinpoints the origin of the last days in Hebrews 1:1-2. Those verses state, *God, who at sundry times and in divers manners spake in time past unto the fathers by the prophets, Hath in these last days spoken unto us by his Son.*

How could He speak by His Son in the last days if Jesus wasn't speaking in the last days? *The last days existed in Jesus' day, because Jesus was preaching then.

In Acts 2:15-21 we have the record of the prophecy made by Joel in Joel 2:28-32 and its fulfillment. The huge crowds on the day of Pentecost were confused as to what was going on. They asked in verse 12, *What meaneth this?* Peter answered this question by quoting Joel 2:28-32. He answered by saying (paraphrased), "What you are seeing right before your very eyes is the fulfillment of Joel's prophecy concerning the last days."

How could it be happening right before their eyes in the

last days if the last days wouldn't start for 2000 years? The proper answer as to when the last days started is during the ministry of Jesus and the apostles.*The perilous days recorded in 2 Timothy 3:1-5 are symptoms of the sick societies which would occur over and over again for the next 2000 years during the church dispensation.

*They are also wrong about our generation not being able to do anything about our spiritual decline into a major apostasy. We can have a national revival in our day, and before this lesson is finished, you will see how.

Wednesday

UNDERSTAND THE TENDENCY OF MAN TO BACKSLIDE

In showing the cycles which man goes through from a good Christian society to one of total immorality, we will use the book of Judges. In the book of Judges we have a perfect illustration of what has happened over and over again in the world. *There were seven periods of revival followed by seven periods of compromise, followed by nominal Christian living, which was a form of religion that ended up in total apostasy. Let's note the procedure of a healthy Christian society backsliding into total apostasy in the book of Judges.

***First, there was strong Christian leadership and preaching.** Under the leadership of Joshua and in obedience to the Law of Moses, God blessed Israel with victory after victory. These victories were recorded in the book of Joshua. Judges 2:7 also tells of true service to God, *And the people served the LORD all the days of Joshua, and all the days of the elders that outlived Joshua, who had seen all the great works of the LORD, that he did for Israel.*

Second, Even before the death of Joshua and the leaders of Israel, compromise had already set in. God had told them not to make a league or associate with the inhabitants of the land, but to drive them all out of the country. *The tribes of Israel began to slack off and failed to obey God's commands. They became allies with their enemy, friends of the world and thus enemies with God (James 4:4).

***Third,** There arose another generation who knew not the Lord. Judges 2:10 states, *and there arose another generation after them, which knew not the LORD, nor yet the works which he had done for Israel.*

Fourth, The children of Israel did evil and turned to false gods (Judges 2:11-13).

***Fifth,** God stopped blessing them and things got worse and worse (Judges 2:14-17).

Sixth, God raised up a judge who delivered them from their sins and enemies (Judges 2:18).

Seven, They followed this pattern seven times, and God delivered them seven times.

Thursday

UNDERSTAND THE BOOK
OF SECOND TIMOTHY

*The book of 2 Timothy was written during the very worst time of the first apostasy. Gone were the days when thousands were being saved. Gone were the days of spirit-filled revivals and churches. It was thirty to forty years after Pentecost, and the first great apostasy had arrived in full force. Churches were compromising and leaving the true faith (Christianity). Other churches were splitting and going into doctrinal error. In 2 Timothy 1:15, Paul refers to much of his life's work being destroyed. He said, *This thou knowest, that all they which are in Asia be turned away from me; of whom are Phygellus and Hermogenes.* Two or three million believers had been deceived and began following false teachers. Since that time Asia has become a dark hole of religion.

Paul was in prison waiting to be executed. Trusted servants were forsaking him, and no one came to his trial when he was sentenced to death (2 Timothy 4:16).

In 2 Timothy 3:1-5 Paul refers to the apostasy they were experiencing as perilous times and then lists the moral corruption existing in his day. *This know also, that in the last days perilous times shall come. For men shall be lovers of their own selves, covetous, boasters, proud, blasphemers, disobedient to parents, unthankful, unholy, Without natural affection, trucebreakers, false accusers, incontinent, fierce, despisers of those that are good, Traitors, heady, highminded, lovers of pleasures more than lovers of God; Having a form of godliness, but denying the power thereof: from such turn away.*

*Notice the last four words in verse five: **From such turn away.** How could Timothy turn away from all those evil things if they did not exist in his day? In addition to Paul's instruction for Timothy to turn away from the evils listed in verses one through five, he describes the actions and the end results of those who practice such things. *Notice Paul's use of **present tense verbs** in verses five through nine:

In verse five we have the present tense verb, TURN.

In verse six we have three present tense verbs: *ARE, CREEP* and *LEAD.*

In verse seven we have the present tense verb, *LEARNING.*

In verse eight we have two present tense verbs: *DO* and *RESIST.*

These present tense verbs indicate that the conditions listed in verses one through five **were happening in Timothy's day.** These same *perilous times* would be repeated over and over again when God's people would compromise, become weak, and stop preaching God's

Word with Holy Spirit power. Paul illustrates that the apostasy would pass just like the falling away in Moses' day. He said, *But they shall proceed no further: for their folly shall be manifest unto all men, as theirs also was* (2 Timothy 3:9).

Paul instructed Timothy on what to do during the apostasy.

Paul reminded Timothy that the life of a true preacher was one of danger and trials (2 Timothy 3:10-13). In verse 10 he reminded Timothy of his example of love and victorious life as he lived through many hardships. *He is saying we have been through perilous times before and God has always brought us through. Paul reminds Timothy that He will bring him through the perilous times also. He then instructed Timothy to:

1. Continue in the fundamentals of the faith which **you have been taught** (2 Timothy 3:11-15).

2. Remember the inspired Scripture in which **you have been taught** (2 Timothy 3:16-17).

3. Paul reminds him that among the good works the Bible will fully instruct in is **the good work of how to overcome the apostasy he is in.**

4. He reminded him of the imminent coming of Jesus and reminded him that every one of Timothy's works would be judged (2 Timothy 4:1).

5. *He tells him to **keep preaching the Word** with power and without compromise (2 Timothy 4:2).

After giving these instructions, Paul gives Timothy the inspired method of overcoming the apostasy which WOULD BEGIN A NEW DAY OF REVIVAL.

Friday

UNDERSTAND THE PRINCIPLES OF HOW TO OVERCOME A PERIOD OF APOSTASY

There are four simple steps in overcoming a period of apostasy. *Since they are so simple, the theological minds overlook them. **Most minds are focused on the negative things** which prevail during a falling away and they also overlook them. The traditional mindset that we are in the last days of this age, just before the coming of Jesus, cannot see these four simple principles which are listed in 2 Timothy 4:5.

But watch thou in all things, endure afflictions, do the work of an evangelist, make full proof of thy ministry.

Please note what those four principles are:

- **Watch in all things**
- **Endure afflictions**
- **Do the work of an evangelist**
- **Make full proof of thy ministry**

Please examine more closely what these four principles teach.

FIRST, WATCH THOU IN ALL THINGS

What are some of the *all things* for which one should watch?

1. *Watch for the imminent return of Christ**. He said He would return when least expected. Be working with zeal, love, and compassion when He does come.

2. **Watch your heart**. Don't allow yourself to become discouraged. A leader who allows himself to become discouraged cannot inspire others to follow and sacrifice. **Quit the negative talk** about how hard it is, or how hard your field of labor is. **Negative talk and complaining sow unbelief** in the lives of one's members and will make it harder to develop them in a walk of faith.

3. **Watch for the attacks of the Devil**. The Devil is a bully, and he likes to attack and overwhelm a person when he is weak or down.

4. **Watch over the members who are still true**, especially the young converts. It would be easy for them to get discouraged and quit, or to be led astray by other groups. Remember, they are hurting also.

SECOND, ENDURE AFFLICTIONS

Going through a period of apostasy is tough. One works

so hard only to have little or no results. Paul offers Timothy three things to help him endure the hard times he must go through before he will see revival.

1. Losing members you won and love is heartbreaking, and it hurts, but **it will strengthen and teach you how to walk by faith** if you will let it. Claim God's promise in 1 Peter 5:10, which promises you the victory plus eternal rewards.

2. *Remember, **you are a soldier of Jesus Christ, so endure hardness as a soldier** (2 Timothy 2:3). Crying or complaining will not help anyone, but will only make things worse. As a soldier, buck up and act ye like a man. Fight the good fight of faith; God will bring you through **the dark night to a brighter day that will end in eternal rewards.**

3. **God has promised to work all things together for your eternal good** (Romans 8:28). If you suffer with Him, you will reign with Him in the 1,000-year reign. Remember, you are an eternal being, and He has your eternal good at heart. He has promised that you will win if you faint not.

THIRD, DO THE WORK OF AN EVANGELIST

1. The work of an evangelist **is winning souls.**

2. The work of an evangelist is **preaching Spirit-filled, evangelistic sermons.**

3. The work of an evangelist is **teaching and showing people how to win souls in a classroom setting**. Then the evangelist becomes a soul-winning trainer who takes the trainee out and perfects him in the vocation of winning souls by giving him on-the-job training. He continues this on-the-job training until the trainee becomes a trainer. This brings new life and joy back into the church service, which then begins to attract others.

4. When the pastor begins to do the work of an evangelist, it is slow at first. He may be the only trainer. But as he persists in making the outreach for sinners a training effort also, he has the potential of good growth that can accelerate to a rapid growth. *As the training teams increase, so will the excitement, and success will increase. Bear in mind that the first church only had 120 trainers after three-and-one-half years. But this small group was able to win and train enough converts who grew and reached the whole known world in forty years. As one does the work of an evangelist (trainer), he should remember the first two parts of overcoming an apostasy: **watch in all things and continue to endure during hardness.**

FOURTH, MAKE FULL PROOF
OF THY MINISTRY

1. Making full proof of your ministry **means to incorporate the principle of protecting the new converts you win**. Remember, they learn things like a young child

learns – by observation. **They watch the actions** of the older church members and then begin to imitate their lifestyle. In a period of apostasy, the lifestyle of the average professing Christian is nominal at best. This means we must protect the new convert from careless church members by placing a dedicated church member over them as their role model.

2. **Making full proof of your ministry can be patterned after the practice** revealed in Acts 2:42. We must impress and insist that the members meet the standard of conduct and practice which the Holy Spirit will bless.

3. **What caused this apostasy we are in?** How did we get in this sad shape? After analyzing what caused the apostasy, begin to follow closely the mandate in the Great Commission, and we will be well on our way to a national revival.

Summary: Review the truths of God's Word we covered:

1. God commands each Christian to become a personal soul-winner.

2. God requires that each saved person learn to win souls well enough to train others.

3. God called men into the ministry to lead in training or perfecting Christians to a high level in soul winning and discipling.

4. The first small local church that followed these

principles was able to have massive revival that covered the whole world.

5. Our generation of churches and pastors are under the same mandate as were the first Christians who made up the membership of the first church.

6. **America can be saved** if we get 100 churches and pastors to believe these biblical principles. This statement is based on the fact that most pastors are followers. If 100 churches worked God's program of training, they would see a new spirit of joy in their churches and a tremendous growth. This would attract many of the other churches and pastors, who would soon follow suit.

7. *Judgment is looming on the horizon**. Jesus will be back soon. This will mean that every one of us will stand all alone before Him and give account of our ministry. The Bible still states, *Therefore to him that knoweth to do good and doeth it not, to him it is sin* (James 4:17). The Bible still promises pastors in 1 Peter 5:10 a position of eternal glory if we go through the tough times and obey Him.

The choice is yours. Keep following the traditional lifestyle and **have a very bad hair day** when you stand before Jesus with blood on your hands, or follow the instructions in the Bible to perfect your members to do the work of the ministry and be rewarded by Jesus when you rule and reign with Him for 1000 years in honor!

MONDAY

1. The Bible _____ promises that we can have _____ revival in _____ in our day.

2. God gave the _____ or simple _____ which promise that national revival.

3. America is following in the steps of _____ as was experienced in the land of _____.

4. America is losing _____ _____ of its teenagers within _____ years of graduation from high school.

5. Most of this generation's _____ will suffer in the fires of hell because of the _____ and _____ of their grandparents.

TUESDAY

1. We will clearly show the _____ of man to turn back to _____.

2. First, they are _____ as to when the last days _____.

3. The Bible _____ the origin of the _____ _____ in Hebrews 1:1-2.

4. The last days _____ in Jesus' day, because Jesus was _____ then.

5. The _____ days recorded in 2 Timothy 3:1-5 are symptoms of sick _____.

6. They are also wrong about our _____ not being able to do any-thing about our _____ decline.

WEDNESDAY

1. There were seven periods of _____ followed by seven periods of _____.

2. First, there was strong Christian _____ and _____.

3. The _____ of Israel began to slack off and _____ to obey God's commands.

4. Third, there arose _____ genera-tion who _____ _____ the Lord.

5. Fifth, God stopped _____ them and things got _____and _____ (Judges 2:14-17).

THURSDAY

1. The book of 2 Timothy was written
_____ the very worst time of
the _____ apostasy.

2. Notice the last four words in verse five: *from such*
_____ _____.

3. Notice the _____ _____
_____ which Paul uses in verses five
through nine.

4. He is saying we have been through
_____ times before and God
has _____brought us through.

5. He tells them to keep preaching the Word
with _____ and without
_____ (2 Timothy 4:2).

FRIDAY

1. Since they are _____ _____,
the _____ minds over look them.

2. Watch for the _____
_____ of Christ.

3. Remember, you are a _____ of
Jesus Christ so endure _____ as
a soldier (2 Timothy 2:3).

4. As the training teams _____
so will the _____ and success will _____.

5. Judgment is _____ on the
_____.

DAILY DECLARATION

Lesson Six

Repeat Aloud Each Morning and Evening

I will strive to do my part in bringing about a national revival by obeying the Great Commission.

MEMORY VERSE:

But none of these things move me, neither count I my life dear unto myself, so that I might finish my course with joy, and the ministry, which I have received of the Lord Jesus, to testify the gospel of the grace of God. (Acts 20:24)

CHECK BLOCK AFTER REPEATING

	Mon	Tues	Wed	Thurs	Fri	Sat	Sun
A.M.							
P.M.							

I will strive to do all that I can. That is all I can do.

Name   **Grade**

LESSON SEVEN

WHAT WILL HAPPEN IF WE DISOBEY THE GREAT COMMISSION?

Monday

In Mark 16:14-15 we have the emphatic command to one local church to go into all the world and preach the gospel to every creature.

In Matthew we have the dual command to the disciples who had been taught to fish for men or win souls. The first command stated, as you go make men into disciples. The second part of the command shows the extent to which the disciples (members of the church) were to train their converts. *The training was to be to the level where their converts could train other Christians to do the work of the ministry.

The third lesson in this series gave the instruction on how one could go through a dark period of apostasy and begin to bring about another spiritual awakening. The simple steps to overcome a period of apostasy and reignite a new period of revival and soul winning were:

- Watch in all things
- Endure afflictions

- Do the work of an evangelist
- Make full proof of the ministry

Today's lesson focuses on the question of *what will happen if people in a dark period of apostasy refuse to follow God's formula for spiritual recovery?

The Scriptures teach that *to him that knoweth to do good and doeth it not, to him it is sin* (James 4:17).

*The Bible also teaches that partial disobedience is still disobedience. These two reminders are to encourage the reader to explore and consider the rest of this lesson.

My question to the reader is: Could you be saved from hell and go to heaven had Jesus not died? Your answer would understandably be, "Of course not!" What if a person never hears of the love and provision that God manifested by giving His Son on the cross? Paul answers this question for us in Romans 10:14 – *How then shall they call on him in whom they have not believed? and how shall they believe in him of whom they have not heard? *and how shall they hear without a preacher?*

In order to receive a fuller answer, please consider the Great Commission in John 20:21-23 – *Then said Jesus to them again, Peace be unto you: as my Father hath sent me, even so send I you. And when he had said this, he breathed on them, and saith unto them, Receive ye the*

Holy Ghost: Whosesoever sins ye remit, they are remitted unto them; and whosesoever sins ye retain, they are retained.

*The Great Commission in John's gospel is what ignited the great revival under the Moravian brethren which continued for almost one hundred years and sent many missionaries around the world. Under the leadership of our Moravian brethren, this revival is thought to be the closest thing to the great spiritual awakening in the book of Acts that the world has ever seen.

We will follow the outline as presented in the book ***The Great Commission According to Jesus.*** That simple outline is:

Tuesday

I. A vivid presentation of the Commission

II. A vivid postscript to the Commission

III. A vivid interpretation of the Commission

> *Then said Jesus to them again, Peace* be *unto you: as* my *Father hath sent me, even so send I you. And when he had said this, he breathed on* them, *and saith unto them, Receive ye the Holy Ghost: Whosesoever sins ye remit, they are remitted unto them;* and *whosesoever* sins *ye retain, they are retained.* (John 20:21-23)

*The average Christian does not feel any sense of responsibility in carrying out the Great Commission. Many members give some type of mission offering because of the Great Commission, but there seems to be a very few believers who comprehend the magnitude of their personal responsibility to the lost world.

Matthew presented the PROCEDURE for the church to follow in making and developing disciples for world evangelization. Mark tells us the METHOD that must be followed. The individual believer is to witness to those in his individual world. Luke stresses the MESSAGE that must be presented in order to make genuine believers. John presents JESUS as the Son of God. As the Son of God, Jesus felt the tremendous need of the lost, their hopeless plight and the consuming consequences if they died lost. When John presented his view of the Great Commission given by Jesus, *he passed this individual responsibility on to the believer.

Years ago when D. L. Moody was first saved, he was presented to a church board as a candidate for church membership. He was asked the question, "What has Jesus done for you in particular?" Young Dwight, who was nervous and untaught in the Scriptures, replied, "I know He has done a lot for us in general, but I cannot think of anything He has done for me in PARTICULAR."

Apostle John's account of the Great Commission *takes

the responsibility of the believer out of the general category and makes the individual believer feel his responsibility to a lost world in PARTICULAR.

I. A VIVID PRESENTATION
OF THE COMMISSION

*A. In the question, **"WHAT WOULD JESUS DO?"** John shows his insight into his job as a Christian by saying, "My job on earth is the same job God the Father gave His Son to do while He was on the earth."

B. AS MY FATHER SENT ME

1. Why did God the Father send Jesus into the world? Jesus answers this question in Luke 19:10, *For the Son of man is come **to seek and to save** that which was lost.*

2. The daily life of Jesus demonstrates why He came into the world.

a. He won Nicodemus, the woman at the well, Zacharias, the thief on the cross, and hundreds of others in His daily life.

b. He was teaching, developing, and encouraging others daily.

c. Jesus sacrificed His life.

1. *Even so send I you.* This is very clearly stated. *"I,

Jesus, am sending you to do the same things and for the same reason that my Father sent me."

2. *Even so* comes from the Greek *Houtos Kai*, which means "in the same manner" or "in the manner previously described or illustrated."

3. The Great Commission, according to John, simply bypasses laws, procedures, and technicalities, and speaks directly to the believer's heart. Whatever Jesus did in a given situation is the same thing you should do. Jesus was totally committed to the SAVING of lost souls and to the development of believers.

4. We need to die to self and present our body as a living sacrifice (Romans 12:1).

Wednesday

II. A VIVID POSTSCRIPT TO THE COMMISSION

A. THE AVERAGE REACTION TO THE COMMISSION.

1. Well, Jesus was divine; I am human. He was perfect and I am imperfect. I know that verse said that, *but you really can't expect me to GIVE UP everything and become a religious fanatic, can you?

2. I will give some to missions. I believe if I do, God

will understand. I will go to church myself. I can only answer for myself.

*3. If I get a chance, I will witness to some of my friends or even to some of the people I meet. I will pass out some tracts. I do pray for missionaries – when I remember.

B. THE POSTSCRIPT TO JOHN'S COMMISSION.

1. It seems as if Jesus anticipated all of our human reasoning and excuses because He added a postscript to the Great Commission.

2. Stated in verse 23:

> *Whosoever sins ye remit, they are remitted unto them; and whosoever sins ye retain, they are retained.* (John 20:23)

*C. HOW DOES MAN HAVE POWER TO REMIT SINS?

*1. The postscript to the Great Commission teaches that man has power to remit sins. But the question arises, "How does man have power to remit sins?"

2. As the believer goes and presents the plan of salvation, prays for the sinner, and persuades him to call upon the name of Jesus, then his sins are remitted.

3. If the believer fails to go, if he fails to pray, if the

believer fails to persuade the sinner to call upon the Saviour's name, then the sinner's sins are retained and HE GOES TO HELL.

*4. This postscript shows the believer what his responsibility toward the lost really is. It also shows him that both God and the sinner need the believer to turn away from his normal religious life to dedicate and imitate the life of Jesus.

Thursday

III. A VIVID INTERPRETATION OF THE COMMISSION

A. PAUL WAS PURE FROM THE BLOOD OF ALL MEN. *Wherefore I take you to record this day, that I am pure from the blood of all* men. *For I have not shunned to declare unto you all the counsel of God* (Acts 20:26-27).

1. **What does it mean**, *Pure from the blood of all men?* This phrase is defined in Ezekiel 3:18. God told Ezekiel that *if he didn't warn the sinners and they died in their sins, then Ezekiel would **have their blood on his hands.** If he tried to win them and they would not listen, then they were responsible for their own condition and Ezekiel WAS PURE FROM THEIR BLOOD.

2. **Paul said he was pure from their blood because** he had declared unto them the whole counsel of God. He

had warned them night and day with tears for the space of three years (Acts 20:31).

B. ISRAEL HAD THE BLOOD OF THE SOULS OF THE POOR INNOCENTS IN THEIR SKIRTS. *Also in thy skirts is found the blood of the souls of the poor innocents; I have not found it by secret search, but upon all these* (Jeremiah 2:34). *The Jews in **Jeremiah's day were much like the better church members who are alive today.**

- They went to church faithfully.

- They lived good, moral lives.

- They tithed or gave to the Lord.

- They identified themselves as believers to family or friends, but they did not witness to them. *Because they failed to obey their personal responsibility to witness, God rejected them.

But please examine what God thought of their moral, self-centered lives.

1. They were charged with their blood and were rejected by God (Jeremiah 2:32-37).

*2. **The Jews pleaded that they lived a clean life** and were living morally (Jeremiah 2:35).

3. **God rejected this argument** and told them they

were guilty by asking them this question, *hast thou also taught the wicked ones thy ways?* (Jeremiah 2:33).

Friday

*C. DAVID PLEADED WITH GOD TO DELIVER HIM FROM BLOOD GUILTINESS.

1. *Deliver me from bloodguiltiness, O God...* (Psalms 51:14). He promised that he would go back to soul winning if God would honor his request (Psalms 51:13), but David died with the blood of innocent people on his hands. In 2 Samuel 18:33, David mourns over his son Absalom who died and went to hell. David continues to mourn in 2 Samuel 19 and for the rest of his life, because he had the blood of his own son on his hands. David was comforted when his infant son died by the knowledge that *I can go where he is* [heaven] (2 Samuel 12:23), but wept uncontrollably when Absalom went to hell. *This is one of the most horrible possibilities that many parents face today. Oh, what a fearful, heartbreaking experience many parents have at the judgment seat where they will face their lost children and see them cast into hell.

D. THEIR LIVES PROVED THEY FELT THEIR RESPONSIBILITY TO THE LOST.

1. Paul persuaded men. He knew the terror of the Lord and persuaded them (2 Corinthians 5:11). * [He became]

OBEYING THE GREAT COMMISSION

all things to all men, that I might by all means SAVE SOME (1 Corinthians 9:22, emphasis added).

2. Jude pulled (snatched) them out of the fire (hell) (Jude 23).

3. Jesus said, … *compel them to come in* …(Luke 14:23).

4. The early disciples fasted and prayed night and day because they wanted to fulfill their responsibility to the Commission and to the lost.

5. We are commanded to go!

a. If you go, **you will be rewarded**. Please read and study the great rewards found later in this book.

b. If you ignore the command and do not go, then you will have blood on your hands.

E. ARE YOU JUDGING YOURSELF BY COMPARING YOURSELF TO OTHERS OR TO THE BIBLE?

1. Although Paul warned believers not to compare themselves with other friends and Christians who lived around them, most of us still do it. In comparing ourselves to others, we believe that if we are doing as well or better than those around us, we will make out pretty well at the judgment seat of Christ.

2. God deals with this comparison in the book of James,

where He informs believers what to expect when they, as individuals, stand before the Lord and have their lives and works judged.

3. Each of us would be wise if we memorize the verse that gives this clear distinction. It states, *For he shall have judgment without mercy, that hath shewed no mercy; and mercy rejoiceth against judgment* (James 2:13).

4. Note the clear warning, *He* [God] *shall have judgment without mercy, THAT HATH SHEWED NO MERCY.* This meant that when a believer who lives among sinners who are condemned to spend eternity in hell, shows no mercy by attempting to get them saved, he will receive no mercy from the Lord when he stands before Him at the judgment seat. The believer who was self-centered while living his life and had no mercy toward the lost world will find an angry judge who will severely sentence the self-centered believer.

5. But the Lord is quick to add, *and mercy rejoiceth against judgment.* This means the believer who obeys the Commission, *as my Father hath sent me, even so send I you,* and has given his life to helping sinners get saved will have a good day and rejoice when he stands at the judgment seat of Christ.

6. One reaps what he sows. Sow obedience and show mercy toward the lost and dying people and reap mercy when you stand before the Lord. But oh! Those who do

not sow mercy will receive no mercy! They will bear this memory and the consequences of a self-centered life throughout the thousand year reign. It is only after the millennial reign in Revelation 21:4 that God will wipe away all tears from our eyes, and the former things are forgotten.

F. WHAT IF?

1. What if Jesus had not died on the cross? The correct answer is, "We would be hopelessly lost in sin, condemned to hell."

2. What if you will not die to self and accept your personal responsibility to the lost?

SUMMARY: The Bible stresses method as much as it teaches doctrine. Christianity is not philosophy. Christianity is a way of life, the believer's new vocation. The Great Commission, according to John, speaks not to people in general, but to the individual **in particular**. He edifies the believer's job *as He tells him that he has the power to either remit or retain sin.

A question to each heart, "Do you accept the Great Commission as a philosophy or as a pattern for you to follow, as a way of life?

MONDAY

1. The training was to be to the level where their _____ could train other Christians to do the work of the

_____.

2. What will happen if people in a _____ period of apostasy _____ to follow God's formula for spiritual _____?

3. The Bible also teaches that _____ _____ is still _____.

4. *"...And how shall they* _____ _____ *a preacher?"*

5. The Great Commission in _____ gospel is what ignited the great revival under the _____ brethren.

TUESDAY

1. The average Christian does not feel any sense of _____ in carrying out the Great

_____.

2. He _____ this _____ responsibility on to the _____.

3. Takes the responsibility of the believer out of the
_____ category and makes the
individual believer _____ his responsibility.

4. SUMMED UP IN THE QUESTION,
"
_____ _____ _____
_____?"

5. "I, Jesus, am sending you to do the _____
things for the _____ reasons that my
_____ sent _____".

WEDNESDAY

1. But you really can't expect me to _____
_____ everything and become a religious
_____, can you?

2. If I get a chance, I will _____ to
some of my _____.

3. HOW DOES MAN HAVE _____
TO _____ SINS?

4. The _____ to the Great
Commission _____ that man has
power to remit sins.

5. This postscript shows the _____
what is responsibility toward the lost _____ is.

THURSDAY

1. If he didn't _____ the sinners and they _____ in their sins, then Ezekiel would have their _____ on his _____.

2. The Jews in _____ day were much like the _____ church members who are alive today.

3. Because they _____ to obey their _____ responsibility to witness, God _____ them.

4. The Jews pleaded that they lived a _____ life and were living _____ (Jeremiah 2:35).

5. ...*hast thou also taught the* _____ *ones thy* _____? (Jeremiah 2:33).

FRIDAY

1. David pleaded with God to _____
him from _____ guiltiness.

2. This is one of the most _____
possibilities that many _____ face today.

3. [He became] *all things to all men, that I might by all
means* _____ _____(1 Corinthians
9:22).

4. … *he* [God] *shall have* _____
without _____, *that hath showed* _____
mercy (James 2:13).

5. As He tells him that he has the power to either
_____ or _____ sin.

DAILY DECLARATION

Lesson Seven

Repeat Aloud Each Morning and Evening

Jesus suffered the pains of hell that I may give my life in telling others of His love.

MEMORY VERSE:

Wherefore, my beloved, as ye have always obeyed, not as in my presence only, but now much more in my absence, work out your own salvation with fear and trembling (Philippians 2:12).

CHECK BLOCK AFTER REPEATING

	Mon	Tues	Wed	Thurs	Fri	Sat	Sun
A.M.							
P.M.							

I accept that I may have the blood of poor lost sinners on my hands if I do not witness to them.

Name   Grade

LESSON EIGHT

THE GREAT COMMISSION OFFERS HOPE FOR THE PRESENT SUFFERING OF THE DYING MASSES

Monday

PART ONE

Death is all around us! *Hurting, struggling people are all around us, but most of us choose not to see them. I will not try to use statistics to prove that point, because most people who are living would be more convinced we are in the last days and cannot change our day. But in our life's manual, the Holy Bible, God has promised, *My sheep hear my voice,* or words (John 10:27). I will develop this lesson using three headings:

I. The Cause of the Suffering Masses

II. The Cries of the Suffering Masses

III. The Cure for the Suffering Masses

I. THE CAUSE FOR THE SUFFERING MASSES

In the verse prior to the Great Commission found in the gospel of Mark, we find the cause for the suffering masses.

Jesus was very angry at His disciples who had rejected the testimony of the ones He had sent to inform them of His resurrection. He had sent not one, but two messengers to report that He was alive. Their response to the exciting announcement that Jesus was alive was totally rejected by the apostles, who were huddled together in fear between locked doors. Suddenly Jesus appeared in the midst. The verse stated that He was angry with them. In fact, the word that revealed His anger is *upbraided*. Webster's dictionary defines the word *upbraided* as "to pull, shake, to scold or chide for some wrongdoing; to reprove." This word indicates the anger Jesus had toward the apostles as He gave them a tongue lashing for the sins which cause the hurting of the suffering masses. The two sins that cause the hurting of the suffering masses as *revealed in Mark 16:14 **are the sins of unbelief and hardness of heart.**

These two major sins are what plague all of God's children. *Unbelief is what causes God's people to draw back to their personal destruction (Hebrews 10:38-39).

*Unbelief is caused when people get their eyes upon

themselves and their human weakness. They become afraid of what others will say or think. The Devil begins to build doubts and insecurities in their minds until they never obey God to fulfill His purpose for their lives.

*Hardness of heart is caused by the selfish, self-centered pursuit of a man who wants to have things for his own self-gratification. He refuses to even consider or think about the needs of the lost world. In his hardness of heart, he even refuses to consider the pain and suffering of those all around him. If he even thinks about it at all, he reasons that the people who are suffering brought the suffering upon themselves and does nothing about it.

We know there is a cure for man's unbelief and hardness of heart, because of the ministries of the twelve apostles later in life. They literally became great men of faith and courage as they pursued God's command to go into all the world and preach the gospel to every creature. We will reveal the cure for the sins of unbelief and hardness of heart later in this lesson.

Tuesday

II. THE CRIES OF THE SUFFERING MASSES

I confess that I do not have the words to describe the suffering of the masses on the earth today. My only hope is that the Holy Spirit will bless the Word and my feeble efforts.

A. Meditate on Jeremiah's description of the suffering of his fellow man in the eighth chapter of Jeremiah.

Can you imagine the heartbreak of the poor people who said in Jeremiah 8:15,*We looked for peace, but no good came; and for a time of health, and behold trouble!*

In that verse Jeremiah describes people looking for peace and a solution to their problem, only to be disappointed when more trouble came and things got worse. This same generation looked for better health for a loved one, only to have that person get worse and die. They continued in their suffering and then uttered, *When I would comfort myself against sorrow, my heart is faint in me* (Jeremiah 8:18).

In verse 18, he describes a person who was attempting to comfort himself. He was only looking for a little ray of hope, but alas, none came, and he was overwhelmed by sorrow.

In verse 19, he describes the loneliness that grips the

heart of so many of the world's population. When they cannot fill that longing and emptiness, *they turn to idols and cry out in despair, *Isn't there any God of comfort?*

In Jeremiah 8:20, Jeremiah utters one of the saddest statements ever made by a hurting, scared human being. His heartbreaking words are *The harvest is past, the summer is ended, and we are not saved.* This heartbreaking verse describes the masses that live their entire lives struggling to find peace and the real purpose of life, only to fail. As they face their tragic end, *they realize that whatever life was, they had missed it and now are dying lost.

In verse 21, Jeremiah describes the hurt he is suffering for his generation of perishing people. He said, *For the hurt of the daughter of my people am I hurt; I am black; astonishment hath taken hold on me.*

In Jeremiah 9:1, he utters the words of how the suffering of the lost people in his generation affected him. *Oh that my head were waters, and mine eyes a fountain of tears, that I might weep day and night for the slain of the daughter of my people!*

*He felt so helpless in his attempt to come to their aid that he wanted to flee to some far-off place where he would not see or feel their sufferings anymore (Jeremiah 9:2).

B. Isaiah weeps over his day. After Isaiah's conversion

he volunteered to go and preach to the lost. His very words of commitment still ring in the ears of this modern generation. He said to the Lord, *Here am I; send me* (Isaiah 6:8).

Wednesday

Isaiah's words of warning are not nearly as well known. Of all the preachers, prophets, or apostles in the Bible, *Isaiah spoke more about hell than any other person except Jesus. One of the most soul-searching verses is Isaiah 33:14, where he asks a heart-rending question. After referring to the petrifying fear of the sinners of his day and the horrifying surprise of the false professors, he asks the question about the consuming torment of those who are lost. His very words were, *The sinners in Zion are afraid; fearfulness hath surprised the hypocrites. *Who among us shall dwell with the devouring fire? Who among us shall dwell with everlasting burnings?*

*There were no words of comfort or anything anyone could do to come alongside Isaiah when he observed the dying masses, because *he knew their end would never come as they suffered the horrors of hell. Visualize the grief he was feeling when he uttered these words, *Therefore said I, Look away from me; *I will weep bitterly, labour not to comfort me, because of the spoiling of the daughter of my people* (Isaiah 22:4).

Thursday

*C. In Ecclesiastes 5:1 Solomon, the wise man, spoke of the futility the masses faced in his day. He referred to the tears of the oppressed and to the fact they had no comforter or any place to turn for relief in their hopeless situation. *He said they are hopelessly caught in their futile life with no power to escape or any way to make things better. He even spoke humanly by saying in verse 2 that *he thought those who were dead were better off than those who were hopelessly suffering in their oppression. His exact words are recorded in Ecclesiastes 4:1-2: *So I returned, and considered all the oppressions that are done under the sun: and behold the tears of such as were oppressed, and they had no comforter; and on the side of their oppressors there was power; but they had no comforter. Wherefore I praised the dead which are already dead more than the living which are yet alive.*

He later spoke the immortal words recorded in Proverbs 11:30, which reveal man's real purpose on this earth: *The fruit of the righteous is a tree of life; and he that winneth souls is wise.*

D. The psalmist speaks of man's hopeless heartbreak and helplessness in Psalm 142. *He said that his situation overwhelmed him. He complained that his enemies had laid a snare for him to fall into. He said that he searched despairingly for someone to help him. Then he confessed that all of his resources had failed him, and *he felt the futility of being alone **because no man cared for his soul**. His very words were *I looked on my right hand, and beheld, but there was no man that would know me: refuge failed me; no man cared for my soul* (Psalm 142:4).

Friday

E. The brutish man pleads for help. *The brutish man is a lost man who has no spiritual insight, but realizes that something is dreadfully wrong in his life. In Proverbs 30:2-3, he describes his condition when he confesses his condition: *Surely I am more brutish than any man, and have not the understanding of a man. *I neither learned wisdom, nor have the knowledge of the holy.*

*Then in the following verse he pleads for someone to help him. He said, "Who is it that was resurrected and what does that mean? What is His Son's name? Oh, please help me. Tell me the truth before I die." In his despair, pleading for help, he received a rebuke from a religious person (vs. 5-6, paraphrased).

He did not receive any answer, and as far as we know, he died in darkness and now lifts up his eyes in hell.

When Lewis and Clark made their trek from St. Louis, Missouri, to the West Coast, they encountered many friendly Indians. The Indians were impressed by the advancements that the white men had made over their primitive culture. When they asked the reason for this obvious advancement, they were told it was because of the teachings found in the Bible. The various tribes then sent a group of Indians back with Lewis and Clark to get someone to come and teach them from the "white man's book." One of their committee died on the return to St. Louis. After months word came to Lewis and Clark that the Indians were leaving on their trip back to the Northwest. When the Indians were asked why they were leaving, they gave the following answer: "we were sent by our people to find someone to come back to our lands and teach us about the God of the white man's book. You have been very kind to us. You have even showed us houses where the white man's God lives (church buildings), *but no one has told us about the white man's God. Now we will return over the trail for many moons to the land of our people. Long before we get there, people from all of our tribes will gather. We will sit down in silence in the council with them without the white man's book." ***One by one they will all get up and go out into the darkness without the white man's book or his God.**

This illustrates what millions of brutish people are doing all over the world today.

MONDAY

1. _____, struggling people are all around us, but most of us _____ not to see it.

2. Revealed in Mark 16:14 are the sins of _____ and _____ of _____.

3. Unbelief is what causes God's people to _____ back to their personal _____ (Hebrews 10:28-29).

4. Unbelief is caused when people get their eyes upon _____ and their human _____.

5. Hardness of heart is caused by the _____, _____ pursuit of man.

TUESDAY

1. *We looked for* _____, *but no good came, and for a time of health, and behold* _____*! (Jeremiah 8:15)*

2. They turn to _____ and cry out in despair, *Isn't there any God of* _____?

3. The harvest is _____, the summer is ended, and we _____ _____ _____ (Jeremiah 8:20).

4. They realize that whatever life was, they had _____ it and now are _____ lost.

5. He felt so _____ in his attempt to help them that he wanted to _____ to some far-off place.

WEDNESDAY

1. Isaiah spoke more about _____ than any other person except _____.

2. *Who among us shall dwell with the* _____ _____?

3. There were no words of _____ or _____ anyone could do.

4. He knew their end would _____ come as they _____ the horrors of _____.

5. *I will weep _____, labour not to _____ me.*

THURSDAY

1. Solomon, the wise man, spoke of
the _____ that the
_____ faced in his day.

2. He said they are _____ caught
in their futile life with no _____ to escape.

3. He thought that those who were _____
were better off than those who were
_____ suffering.

4. He said that his _____
overwhelmed _____.

5. He felt the futility of being _____ because
no man _____ for his soul.

FRIDAY

1. The _____ man is a lost man who
has no _____ insight.

2. *I neither _____ wisdom, nor have*
the _____ of the _____.

3. Then in the following verse he _____
for someone to _____ him.

4. But no one has told us about the _____
man's _____.

5. One by one they will all get up and go out into the
_____ without the white man's
book or his _____.

DAILY DECLARATION

Lesson Eight

Repeat Aloud Each Morning and Evening

I will strive to follow the example of Jesus, who was moved with compassion in order to help the hurting masses.

MEMORY VERSE:

We looked for peace, but no good came; and for a time of health, and behold trouble! (Jeremiah 8:15)

CHECK BLOCK AFTER REPEATING

	Mon	Tues	Wed	Thurs	Fri	Sat	Sun
A.M.							
P.M.							

I praise the Lord for his goodness to me and my family. I will strive to bring that same blessing to others.

_____

Name   Grade

LESSON NINE

HOPE FOR THE PRESENT SUFFERING OF THE DYING MASSES

Monday

PART TWO

GOD OFFERS A CURE AND IS SEEKING MEN

God's description of man's life. God was so moved by the horrible plight of rebellious, brutish man that He gave His Son to die in each man's place to pay for his sins. This opened the way for the redemption of each human being ever born on this earth.

God described the condition of fallen man and his trouble in Job 14:1: *Man that is born of a woman is of few days, and full of trouble.*

*As soon as Adam sinned, God came searching for him. He told him of His loving provision for Adam and the human family. He then clothed Adam in the skin of the innocent lamb he had slain. This lamb was the perfect picture of the innocent, perfect Son of God and His sacrifice for man's sin on the cross.

Since that day, God has been searching for the brutish man. In the Old Testament He chose Abraham and his people to seek and to find fallen man. In the New Testament, *He founded and commissioned His church to lead in the search for lost man. But His effort to save the people of various countries is illustrated by the lack of success He had in Ezekiel's day. In Ezekiel's day we have these words penned, *And I sought for a man among them, that should make up the hedge, and stand in the gap before me for the land, that I should not destroy it: but I found none. Therefore have I poured out mine indignation upon them; I have consumed them with the fire of my wrath: their own way have I recompensed upon their heads, saith the Lord GOD* (Ezekiel 22:30-31).

The struggling masses of this world are still crying out for relief and for help. Will we as Americans hear their desperate cries and respond, or will God have to pen the sad, tragic words which Ezekiel wrote so many years ago over our decaying corpses?

*He is still searching for a man to stand in the gap for America. Will you be that man? Will you echo the response that Isaiah made when he made a total surrender to God? Will you say, "Here am I Lord, send me"?

Oh, my dear friend, please respond to the desperate cries of those around you! *Don't look at people in a careless way. Look at them as hurting people who need Jesus. *These eternal beings will soon be in the eternal fires of hell unless we win them.

Tuesday

III. THE CURE FOR THE SUFFERING MASSES

Just as the Bible reveals the cause for the suffering of the lost masses, it also reveals the cure. The two main causes for the suffering of the masses are unbelief on the part of God's people and *the hardness of their hearts toward the need of those around them.

1. *The cure for unbelief is faith. *Faith cometh by hearing and hearing by the Word of God* (Romans 10:17).

*God promises to give the believer enabling grace from His rich source of *all grace* (1 Peter 5:10). He has stated through His most tested servant who suffered more than any other preacher in the New Testament that His grace was sufficient for every situation (2 Corinthians 12:9). *But man does not believe God and draws back in unbelief.

God promises to give man wisdom (James 1:5). *This means God will loose man's tongue and teach him what to say. He will cause man to grow in grace and in the knowledge of the Lord (2 Peter 3:18). Through tribulations He will cause man to grow to the level where experience has taught him wisdom (Romans 5:1-5).

Wednesday

*God has promised to give man power through the Holy Spirit. This is God's own divine power which the Holy Spirit imparts to the believer in order to equip the worker to succeed in life. He promises never to leave the believer (Hebrews 13:5) and was sent to empower the worker to do God's work (Acts 1:8).

The one major purpose of the Holy Spirit is to aid man in his effort to fulfill God's command of preaching the gospel to the hurting, lost masses of the world.

2. *The cure for the hardness of man's heart is compassion. Please read this promise of a cure offered for the hurting masses: *And of some have compassion, making a difference* (Jude 22).

Notice the upfront promise in verse 22: *And of some have compassion, MAKING A DIFFERENCE.* Compassion will soften the hard heart and cure the spirit of unbelief. The reader may ask the question, "Why will compassion be able to cure the unbelief and hardness of a human heart?" *The answer is in understanding what compassion is and who the hurting people are.

The definition and how the word *compassion* is used *is probably the only cure for unbelief and the hardness of a self-centered heart. Couple this with the statement, *And others save with fear, pulling them out of the fire* [fires of Hell] (Jude 23).

Thursday

1. **The definition of compassion.** The definition of compassion is to have love, pity, and sympathy to such an overwhelming degree that *one is moved to do something, regardless of the personal cost or danger.

2. **God was so moved by compassion** as He looked down upon the masses of suffering people that *He was compelled to give His only begotten Son to die in their place. By making His Son a sin offering, He made a way to reconcile rebellious man back to Himself.

3. **Notice the statement in verse 23.** Others were moved by fear, hating even the deplorable and dangerous situation of those who were as good as in hell. They were compelled to do something about it. They literally began to snatch them out of the burning fires of hell. *Their attention was taken off themselves and was totally focused on the danger of the lost people who were heading to hell. John 3:18 states that people who do not believe in Jesus as their Saviour are condemned already (to hell). John 3:36 goes on to say, *he that believeth not the Son shall not see life, but the wrath of God abideth on him.* These two verses teach that the lost sinner is condemned and is basically already in hell.

4. **The physical sufferings of the peoples** of the world are nothing compared to the sufferings which they will have to endure once they die in a lost condition. *Most

people never stop to consider this ultimate end of their loved ones, especially the sufferings of those in the world.

5. **The question arises** of how could God cause man to have compassion toward his fellow man? How could God cause man to have an understanding that compassion is to have love, pity and sympathy to such an overwhelming degree that *he is compelled to do something about it, regardless of personal cost or danger?

Friday

6. **This question is answered when one understands** how the word is used in the Bible. The word *compassion* is used in two ways:

***First, it is used by God toward fallen man**. God was moved by compassion toward both the present and eternal suffering of the masses to the extent He sacrificed his Son on the cruel cross.

Second, the word *compassion is used by man toward the dearest person in his immediate family. Man may not be moved by the needs of a total stranger, *but man will be moved (by fear) if his dear mother, child, or spouse is in imminent danger. He will not consider his personal danger if his child is drowning in a raging river. He will jump right in and do everything possible in his power to save him. He will not consider any personal needs or limitations. *He is compelled by compassion to save the child's life. The only thing wrong with this illustration is that the people of his family are lost, condemned, and essentially in hell. The way compassion is used, it doesn't see strangers in danger of going to hell, but sees the face of that dear loved one already in the fires of hell. This will overcome the unbelief. This vision will overcome the hardness of his heart and compel him to do everything within his power to snatch that loved one from the fires of eternal hell.

Reader, listen to me! These words are not just part of a preacher's sermon or lesson. The way the word *compassion* is used is from God himself, and it is directed to this generation of believers and pastors who are committing the horrible sins of unbelief and have a hard heart toward the hurting masses of the world. If you begin to practice looking at the lost people of the world as though they were your own flesh and blood and in imminent danger of dying and going to hell, it will soften your hard heart and GET YOUR FOCUS on their dangerous condition. You will get your mind off yourself and be compelled to do God's will for your life! *It would constrain you to do everything in your power to obey God's Great Commission. He still commands, *Go ye into all the world and preach the gospel to every creature.* In injecting how the word *compassion* is used, it causes the person not to look upon every creature as a stranger, but to look upon them as the one dearest to his heart.

MONDAY

1. As soon as _____ sinned, God came
_____ for him.

2. He _____ and _____ His
church to lead in the search for _____ _____.

3. He is still _____ for a man to
stand in the gap for _____.

4. Don't _____ at people in a _____ way.

5. These _____ beings will soon be in the
_____ fires of hell unless we win them.

TUESDAY

1. The _____ of their hearts toward
the _____ of those around them.

2. The _____ for unbelief is _____.

3. God promises to give the believer _____
_____.

4. But man does not _____ God and
_____ back in unbelief.

5. This means God will _____ man's
_____ and teach him what to say.

WEDNESDAY

1. God has _____ to give man _____ through the _____ _____.

2. The _____ for the hardness of man's heart is _____.

3. *And of some have* _____, *MAKING A* _____.

4. The answer is in _____ what compassion is and _____ the hurting people are.

5. Is probably the only _____ for unbelief and the hardness of a _____-_____ heart.

THURSDAY

1. One is _____ to do something, _____ of the personal cost or _____.

2. He was _____ to give His only _____ Son to die in their place.

3. Their attention was taken off_____ and was totally _____ on the danger of the lost people.

4. Most people never stop to _____
this _____ end of their loved ones.

5. He is compelled to do _____
about it, regardless of _____
_____ or danger?

FRIDAY

1. First, it is _____ by God _____
fallen man.

2. Second, the word _____ is
used by _____ toward the dearest person in his
_____ family.

3. But man will be moved (_____ _____)
if his dear mother, _____, or spouse is in imminent danger.

4. He is _____ by compassion to
_____ the child's life.

5. It would constrain you to do _____
in your _____ to obey God's _____
Commission.

DAILY DECLARATION

Lesson Nine

Repeat Aloud Each Morning and Evening

Compassion moved Jesus to give his life. May that same spirit be found in me.

MEMORY VERSE:

And of some have compassion, making a difference: And others save with fear, pulling them out of the fire; hating even the garment spotted by the flesh. (Jude 22-23)

CHECK BLOCK AFTER REPEATING

	Mon	Tues	Wed	Thurs	Fri	Sat	Sun
A.M.							
P.M.							

I will strive to look at others through the eyes of compassion.

_____

Name   **Grade**

LESSON TEN

THE ETERNAL SUFFERINGS OF THOSE WHOM THE GREAT COMMISSION DID NOT REACH

Monday

Think about suffering from a bad toothache that you couldn't get to stop aching. Do you remember the excruciating pain each time your heart beat? Say the tooth became abscessed and sent poison all through your body until the pain in your body was so great that the toothache seemed minor. Your whole body ached and throbbed until you had to scream. But nothing you could do would ease the pain. Multiply your time of suffering by ten million years with no relief in sight, and you have a little insight concerning the suffering in hell.

I was witnessing to a ninety-one-year-old man who was lost and in intensive care, but he had refused to let his family talk to him about the Lord. The medical staff had worked furiously to bring him back out of a coma. God had blessed their efforts. The old man was suffering intense pain.

He yelled at me, "Didn't they tell you that I don't talk about things like that?" (meaning salvation).

"Yes, but you are dying, and because you are lost, will soon be in hell."

"I'm in hell now," he screamed.

I shouted right back, "No you are not!"

"Yes I am. You don't know how bad I am hurting!"

"You are right. I don't know how bad you are hurting, *but there is no pain on earth as bad as the pain in hell. God loves you and He wants to save you from hell."

He interrupted me, "If God loves me like you say He does, then why does He let me suffer like I am suffering?"

I responded, "I heard the doctor tell the nurse to give you a shot for pain when I came in. But what difference does it make? *There won't be any shots in hell to ease your pain. If you are so determined to die and go to hell and refuse any help from God, what difference does it make if you get a shot or not? There will not be any shots for pain in hell. *And the pain you are suffering right now is nothing compared to the pain you will suffer forever and ever in hell."

I hear someone say, "Did you really talk to that old, dying ninety-one-year-old man like that?"

Yes, I talked to an old man like that! Really, what we were doing wasn't talking; it was more like yelling at each other. The family had asked me to get him saved.

God had broken my heart for that dear, old dying man and a sweet, little witness wouldn't faze him. *I was willing to do anything to get him saved. God gave him six more days to live. On the fourth day he was wonderfully saved.

The point of this true story is there is no pain on this earth as bad as the pain in hell, and indescribable pain will continue on and on into the ages. *Revelation 14:11 states they will not have any rest (relief), DAY AND NIGHT FOREVER.

MISPLACED COMPASSION

Tuesday

MISSPENT COMPASSION ON PETS. *We live in a day of misspent compassion. It is said that we spend ten times more money on pets than is given to missions. Now, I love dogs, cats, horses, and all manner of animals. *In this world of stress, betrayal, and loneliness, there is nothing like a pet waiting to love and welcome you home after a tough time. I know, and most pets know, that they are part of the family. God made pets for that very purpose. They are a special gift from God, but they do not possess an eternal soul. Only man was made in the image and likeness of our eternal God and will exist throughout all coming time.

Undoubtedly there will be pets on this earth during the

millennial reign. And we know there will be white horses in heaven, but man is the only eternal being that God created. It was God who gave the Great Commission which we are to obey and be directed by. His message today is still the same as when He first gave it. He said, *Go ye into all the world and preach the gospel to every creature* (Mark 16:15).

When we have compassion on animals and spend more money on them than we spend to get people saved from the eternal fires of hell, **it is a misspent compassion.**

*MISSPENT COMPASSION ON DEALING WITH THE TEMPORAL AND NOT THE ETERNAL.** In our modern day our children must be educated! If parents do not educate their children properly, those children are very likely to struggle the rest of their lives. *But parents should rethink the type of education they give their children. Many send their children off to colleges that are in great conflict with God. That is one of the main reasons that **80 percent of high school graduates quit going to church** within two years of graduation. *Would the same parents send their children to a hostile war without weapons or combat training? There is very little difference in sending their children off to be trained by the enemies of God without a proper Christian foundation. We must teach our children that they are eternal beings and as such will live somewhere, heaven or hell, forever. Therefore, **this misspent compassion** toward our children is aiding this world to destroy their faith and lives.

THE DEFINITION OF GOD'S LOVE

Many of God's children either have never heard the Bible definition of love, or they are willingly ignorant of what God's love is. God gives a very clear definition of what His love is in 1 John 5:3. He said, *For this is the love of God THAT WE KEEP HIS COMMANDMENTS.*

The love of God is not some type of fuzzy feeling.

The love of God is not demonstrated by some emotional outburst or expression.

The love of God is manifested by keeping the commandments of God. The major commandment to each child of God is the Great Commission. The Great Commission commands us to go into all the world and preach (publish, tell or proclaim) the gospel (the good news that God loves sinners and will forgive them if they repent). John made the Great Commission even simpler when he quoted Jesus' words: *As my father hath sent me, even so send I you* (John 20:21).

Most Christian school teachers on all levels of training are very dedicated to enriching and training their students about the mysteries of the world. But these same teachers fail to show the love of God to their students by keeping God's commandment and telling them how to escape the eternal separation from God. This also is a misspent compassion. The end result is simply more educated people in hell.

The same principle applies to medical doctors. They sacrifice greatly in order to help care for their patients, but there will be no injections or any available care to relieve their eternal sufferings in hell. Again, we see misplaced compassion. Unless we tell them about the Great Physician before they die, it is like giving someone something to ease their temporary pain, but ignoring their deadly disease.

Most of God's most faithful saints have a misspent compassion. They love their church, their Bible, and their good way of life, but fail to see what all of their religious activities should be. We are to get the gospel to the lost, then disciple or train them. The Bible still states, *He that winneth souls is wise* (Proverbs 11:30).

THE PHYSICAL SUFFERING IN HELL. When a person is born again, he receives a guarantee from God that he will receive a new, perfect, glorified body. He is saved by God's grace, and by God's grace he will be conformed to the image and likeness of Jesus. But this promise of a new body is not made to those who reject Christ as their Saviour. In fact, the opposite occurs. They will be resurrected from the grave, but they will re-inhabit the same old body that they had when they died. Revelation 20:12-13 reveals this truth. At the white throne judgment only the lost will be judged. God's children have already received a new, glorified, resurrected body.

Paul plainly states this fact in 1 Corinthians 15:38 where he wrote, *But God giveth it a body as it hath pleased him, and to every seed his own body.*

The next few verses describe the differences in glorified bodies which some saints will live in throughout eternity. Then he comes to 1 Corinthians 15:42-44, *So also is the resurrection of the dead. It is sown in corruption; it is raised in incorruption: It is sown in dishonour; it is raised in glory: it is sown in weakness; it is raised in power: It is sown a natural body; it is raised a spiritual body. There is a natural body, and there is a spiritual body.*

Notice the statements, **sown in corruption, sown in dishonor, sown in weakness**, and **sown in a natural body.** What a descriptive way to refer to death. The natural body becomes so corrupt with poison it can no longer function. It gets so weak that the heart and other vital organs cannot continue, and it succumbs to physical death.

Paul is referring to the eternal laws that govern all things. That eternal law states that one reaps what he sows. In death a Christian who lived for the Lord in obedience to the Great Commission dies just like all others die. But in the first resurrection, his body comes forth from the grave in triumph in the form of a beautiful, eternal glorified body. These verses teach that there are various differences in different children of God's eternal, glorified bodies. This is part of the reward that God gives to His children at the judgment seat.

Those who give their lives fully to obeying the Great Commission which states, *preach the gospel to every creature*, will be raised to live eternally in magnificent, glorified bodies. Many of God's people who are living for self will live in glorified bodies that are dull by comparison. This reinforces the principle that what a child of God does in this earthly journey will reflect where he lives and what he will look like in the thousand-year reign.

WHAT ABOUT THE ETERNAL SOULS WHO NEVER GET SAVED?

Wednesday

There is no promise that those who die in unbelief will have a new body. These verses teach the very opposite. God makes it very clear in Revelation 20:11-15 where He talks about the resurrection and judgment of the lost. *God is so angry that heaven and earth flee away from His wrathful countenance. Before Him stand all of His enemies who broke every one of His laws. *They took His mercy and compassion, then with curses and rebellion flung them back into His face. They took the energy and strength *He gave them for good and used it to enslave the poor, trusting masses with false religion.

The time has come for prideful, defiant men who destroyed the faith and corrupted those around them with the poison of unbelief to face God.

Read all of the verses beginning in Revelation 20:11-15, especially looking carefully at verse 13 which states, *And the sea gave up the dead which were in it; and death and hell delivered up the dead which were in them: and they were judged every man according to their works.*

Notice the statement, death (dead bodies) and hell (Hades, where the spirits like the rich man in Luke 16 reside) gave up their dead which were in them. This statement is in perfect harmony with what happens when a lost man dies. *His body begins to decay and return to dust, while his spirit goes to the part of hell (Hades) where he will suffer until his day in court before God at the great white throne judgment, where all lost people must appear.

After the judgment, where a search is made to look for one's name in the Book of Life, and it is not found, the book of his life's works are carefully examined. Bear in mind *these people are standing before God in the same old, corrupted bodies in which they died. After the people in these old, sick, aching bodies are shown every act of consideration and given a chance to prove themselves unworthy of eternal banishment, they are cast into the eternal lake of fire. *And death and hell were cast into the lake of fire. This is the second death* (Rev 20:14).

Death (dead bodies) and hell (Hades, where the eternal spirit has been since their physical death) are cast into the eternal lake of fire to exist forever still in their aching, sickly bodies. Their suffering will be beyond description. But that is only part of their eternal sufferings.

MY UNCLE HOMER'S EXPERIENCE WITH DEATH

Thursday

What kind of bodies will these poor, lost creatures live in for all eternity? In order to try to understand this question better, visualize two dying men. One is saved and the other is lost. One's spirit (the real eternal person) goes to heaven while the lost man goes to the place of departed spirits (Hades). *Both of their bodies decay back to dust. The saved man's body comes forth in a glorified body in the first resurrection, while the lost man's body continues in the grave for another 1000 years. Because he never accepted God's offer of love and mercy, when he is resurrected, he comes up out of his grave in the same condition it was when he died.

My Uncle Homer rebelled against the holy lifestyle of his godly parents. According to his own testimony, he became a hellion. He drank, fought, and committed about every sin a rebellious man could commit.

During World War II, he served his country in the Merchant Marines. He became one of the officers who worked in the engine room. On one of his trips, his ship carried cargo to a port in India. It was during one of that nation's worst famines, where literally millions died. Because of the disease and famine, the captain cancelled all leaves and ordered the crew to stay on the ship. My uncle and the first mate, because of their rank, were an exception and were granted leave.

Later my uncle confessed, "I wished 100 times that I would have stayed on the ship." The things he saw all but poisoned his mind. He said there were dead bodies lying everywhere on the street waiting for a truck to come along and pick them up. He said the sight was so awful that he stayed in the vehicle that they had rented. He watched as the men who worked to pick up the bodies came down the street. They would stack a row of dead bodies on the flatbed of a truck; then they would stack another row of dead or dying bodies in a cross manner on top of the bottom row. Each row of dead bodies was laid in the opposite direction which would hold the other row of dead bodies in place. When the truck could not hold any more corpses, it was driven to a designated spot where the bodies were covered with gasoline and set on fire. On this particular day, the smoke and smell of burning bodies drifted back over the city. He said the smell of death was everywhere.

He said he could not believe what his eyes were seeing. There was a leper colony a few miles out of the city. While he was waiting on the first mate, a truck came from the leper colony and literally dumped the bodies of those who were disfigured by the horrible ravages of leprosy. *He watched those poor creatures as they lay in a pile, some still in the process of dying. One man had only one eye. *The other eye plus much of his face had been eaten away by the awful disease. He lifted the nub of one of his hands that only had part of his fingers still attached. The rest of the pile of human beings resembled something from the garbage pile instead of the bodies of eternal men and women.

His eyes were directed to a man who he thought was dead. *He could see skin worms eating away at the poor man's flesh. But something caused the poor, suffering man to open his eyes. My uncle could not stand the horrible sights any longer, so he went to the bar and forced the first mate to return to the ship. He said that the first thing he did was take a shower in order to get the stench of death off his body. But it did not work. For days he could hardly do his job in the engine room. He would take frequent showers, and at night he had to sleep on the top side of the ship in the fresh, salty air. The horrible, twisted bodies kept coming into his mind, and he kept remembering the taste and smell of death.

In my first revival my Uncle Homer came every night. He fell so under conviction that he could not sleep. He continued to attend, and in the second week of the revival he was gloriously saved. But I have often thought about the masses of people *dying in such old, twisted, diseased bodies such as my uncle described – suffering, unless they were saved, in hell.

But as bad as their suffering is at this very moment in Hades, it will be worse after their old bodies are resurrected from the grave, and they are joined again in that mass of corruption forever.

THE LONELINESS OF THOSE SUFFERING IN HELL

Friday

As a teenager I was a stubborn, headstrong kid who told God, "I don't need you! Stay out of my life!" God took my request seriously, and when my brother, Wayne, was suddenly killed in a car accident, I almost died. *The loneliness and emptiness I experienced were indescribable. I walked around in a stupor. I didn't want to have anything to do with anyone. God had taken me at my word and made no effort to comfort or help me.

King Saul suffered something similar when God withdrew from him. The lonely, empty feeling he experienced caused him to turn to those in the world of darkness for relief. Anything was better than what King Saul was suffering. He would rather know what was going to happen to him than suffer the abandonment of God.

God made man, and in each person He created a place where He, their Creator and God, could live. The life of every lost man is enriched by the blessings that God showers upon all human beings. He blesses them through their family, their works, and the inward hope and purpose which He placed within them. The Bible states that it is the goodness of God that leads men to repentance and to salvation. One could never discover the many ways God is kind and compassionate toward sinful man in order to influence him to be saved. It is God's nature and love that compels Him to be good and kind to sinners.

But when death finally comes to the unregenerate sinner, he is plunged into a world of blackness and emptiness. The longing for God and the depression and futility which follow may be the worst things a sinner experiences in hell. Man has lost the only thing that brought him peace or satisfaction, and this lonely soul will never again have any wholeness, only the dismal feeling of being all alone. *His lonely heart will never again be blessed with hope; it is lost in the lonely blackness of hell in a world of no optimism. Reality strikes him as he realizes that he is in eternal hell, where the pain will never go away.

CONSIDER OTHER HORRIBLE CONSEQUENCES IN ETERNAL HELL

THE POSSIBILITY OF TOTAL ANARCHY

In this world of sin and destruction, it is God and His people who are the salt of the earth and who keep down crime and lawlessness. *Now, the lost live in a world where there is no God or laws to restrain the lawless.

*Will the roving gangs victimize and terrorize these helpless victims? Or will the gang members who are so embittered by sin and crime continually battle and attempt to destroy each other?

Will the people of the nations who have taught their children to hate the people of different cultures come to full fruition? Hell is a world that causes bitterness and hatred to flourish.

How about a world where sex addicts still burn in their lust and are seeking relief from the vile passion by raping others? There is nothing in hell to restrain them.

The possibility that demons will roam in the darkness of hell could make it a more terrifying place. One could only wonder if their intense hate would be unleashed against the human beings who were created in the image and likeness of God, whom they hate. They cannot attack God, but they sure can take out their wrath on man.

What a terrible tragedy that most people in eternal hell lived such a short life on earth where they never found their purpose for existence. They knew something was wrong and turned to empty religion in order to prepare for death. In their search they never found anyone who cared for their soul. They found no genuine peace or lasting fulfillment. There was no comfort, and they struggled in their despairing life until they died. And in hell they will suffer in their old, craving bodies in bitterness and hatred forever. *Why? Because God's people failed to take the Great Commission seriously and take the gospel to them.

THAT'S THE REASON JESUS DIED

The Bible tells a story that illustrates the lost condition of the sinner and his hopeless condition unless the Son of God intervenes.

The story is about the crazed man who lived among the tombs. He would cut himself. He would yell and scream. People had tried to chain him in order to keep him from destroying himself. He was possessed by the Devil. And the summary of all that man could do to help this poor sinner is summed up by the statement, "No man could tame [help] him."

Jesus saw his wounds. Jesus heard his howling and screaming as he lived out among the dead, tormented by the devils which possessed him.

From the throne room in the third heaven Jesus heard his hopeless screams and felt his human sufferings.

Jesus left His royal courtroom, took off His royal clothes, and was born of a virgin in the manger of a stable. He set His face like a flint in order to fulfill His divine purpose to take that poor, lost sinner's place and pay for his sins. As Jesus was on His way to die on the cross, He personally was rowed across a sea to save and set the poor captive free. Then He commanded us to take the gospel to the poor, lost creatures of the world.

Jesus' heart and soul was so into reaching them that He died and paid for each man's sins. Then He depends on us who heard of His love and provision to tell others. He didn't leave it up to just hoping we would share His same love and compassion, especially toward our family and friends. But He pointedly commanded, *GO YE INTO ALL THE WORLD AND PREACH THE GOSPEL TO EVERY CREATURE!*

Failure to obey is rank disobedience, which must be answered to as we stand before God in judgment.

MONDAY

1. But there is no _____ on earth as bad as the _____ in hell.

2. There won't be any _____ in hell to _____ your pain.

3. And the pain you are suffering right now is _____ compared to the pain you will suffer _____ and ever in hell.

4. I was willing to do _____ to get him _____.

5. Revelation 14:11 states they will not have any _____ (relief), _____ AND _____ FOREVER.

TUESDAY

1. We live in a day of _____ _____.

2. In this world of stress, betrayal, and _____, there is nothing like a pet to love and _____ you home.

3. MISSPENT COMPASSION ON DEALING WITH THE _____ AND NOT THE _____.

4. But parents should _____ the type of education they give their _____.

5. Would the same parents send their children to a hostile _____ without _____ or _____ training?

WEDNESDAY

1. God is so _____ that heaven and earth flee away from His _____ _____.

2. They took His _____ and compassion, and with curses and _____, flung them back into His face.

3. He gave them for good and used it to _____ the poor, _____ masses with false religion.

4. His body begins to _____ and return to dust while his _____ goes to the part of hell (_____).

5. These people are standing before God in the same old, _____ bodies in which they _____.

THURSDAY

1. Both of their _____ decay back to _____.

2. He watched those poor _____
as they lay in a _____

3. The other _____ plus much of his _____
had been eaten away by leprosy.

4. He could see skin _____ eating away at the
poor man's _____.

5. Dying in such old, _____,
diseased _____ such as my uncle
_____.

FRIDAY

1. The _____ and _____
I went through were indescribable.

2. His lonely heart will _____ again
be _____ with hope.

3. Now, the lost live in a _____
where there is no _____ or laws to restrain the
_____.

4. Will the roving _____ victimize and
_____ these helpless victims?

5. Why? Because God's people _____
to take the Great Commission _____
and to take the Gospel to them.

DAILY DECLARATION

Lesson Ten

Repeat Aloud Each Morning and Evening

If I give my whole life to educate, feed, clothe, and supply the earthly needs of my family and let them go to hell, I have lost all.

MEMORY VERSE:

For I have five brethren; that he may testify unto them, lest they also come into this place of torment. (Luke 16:28)

CHECK BLOCK AFTER REPEATING

	Mon	Tues	Wed	Thurs	Fri	Sat	Sun
A.M.							
P.M.							

I will give myself totally to seeing that none of my family or friends suffers in hell.

Name   Grade

LESSON ELEVEN

THE PLACE OF TEARS AND COMPASSION IN THE GREAT COMMISSION

Monday

*In our society today, it is not politically correct to use the name of Jesus. One can refer to the higher power, to almighty God, or use any other reference to God, but in some places, it is even against the law to pray in the name of Jesus. Just as it is politically incorrect in politics to use the name of Jesus, *it is religiously incorrect to show any emotion or shed tears in religious services. According to those in the know, shedding tears is a sign of weakness.

But the days are coming when tears will be accepted again, unless we obey the Great Commission and have a national revival.

Tears were in style and perfectly accepted when David and his 600 men returned from a military campaign to find their homes burned to the ground and all of their families taken captive. In fact, *they wept until *they had no more power to weep* (1 Samuel 30:4). Will it take that type of judgment to humble America before tears will come back in style?

As vivid as the statement concerning tears is regarding David and his men weeping until they had no more ability to weep, it is nothing compared to the devastation following the judging hand of God upon the nation of Moab. The total destruction of the nation of Moab is described in the fifteenth chapter of Isaiah. In verse two we have, *He is gone up to Bajith, and to Dibon, the high places, to weep: Moab shall howl over Nebo.* While in verse eight we have these words: *For the cry is gone round about the borders of Moab; the howling thereof unto Eglaim, and the howling thereof unto Beerelim.*

*This howling was more like the wailing of a wounded animal. The pain was so great that a word for intense pain is used to describe the utter pain that caused the devastated people of Moab to weep.

Some of the people who read these words are likely to experience this howling unless we return to obeying the Great Commission.

Oh, what pain and tears there will be at the judgment seat of Christ when one's whole lifetime of works will be burned (1 Corinthians 3:15). These tears will continue for a 1000 years, only to be dried by Jesus after the millennial reign and white throne judgment of God for the lost (Revelation 21:4).

Some of God's people will share the same fate that King David experienced when his son Absalom went to hell. David screamed and wept as he cried, *Oh, my son Absalom, my son, my son Absalom! would God I had died for thee* (2 Samuel 18:33). This remorse and tears followed David to his grave, only to be resurrected again at the judgment seat of Christ. These tears, caused by the failure to get his son Absalom saved, were real then and will be faced again when Absalom is cast into the lake of fire. We know Absalom was lost because of David's actions when his infant son died. David got up, took a bath, and went to church. When asked by his servants why he was so calm after praying, weeping, and fasting for the past several days, David responded, "I can go where he is (Paradise)" (2 Samuel 12:23). But not so with Absalom; there was no hope, just bitter tears.

SOME WEAK MEN OF TEARS

Tuesday

Let's look into God's Word and examine some of the men who would be thought of as weak by our modern standards.

King David, a man after God's own heart. God described David as a man after His own heart. David loved the Lord and lived to serve him. He killed the giant and was a courageous leader of an army.

David explained his burden for the lost when *he said that he watered his couch with tears.

David gave the word on how to be successful in soul winning when he stated that, *They that sow* [the Word] *in tears shall reap in joy* (Psalms 126:5).

David revealed the principle which moved the hand of God when he wrote Psalm 51:17, *The sacrifices of God are a broken spirit: a broken and a contrite heart, O God, thou wilt not despise.* *A broken and contrite heart is a heart that produces tears.

Jeremiah is a prophet many Bible-believing students admire greatly. *He was known as the weeping prophet and was abused and greatly persecuted by his countrymen. In Lamentations 1:12 we have Jeremiah asking the question from his broken heart; *Is it nothing to you, all ye that pass by? Behold, and see if there be any sorrow like unto my sorrow, which is done unto me, wherewith the LORD hath afflicted me in the day of his fierce anger.*

Then we hear the pathos in his voice as he said, *Oh that my head were waters, and mine eyes a fountain of tears,* *that I might weep day and night for the slain of the daughter of my people* (Jeremiah 9:1).

There are many Old Testament prophets who wept over the lost sinners of their day. We will turn our attention to two of the best known preachers in the New Testament era.

Wednesday

Paul, the great missionary, church planter, and inspired writer. In Acts 20:31 we see Paul describe his daily activity which made him such a great soul-winner: *Therefore watch, and remember, *that by the space of three years I ceased not to warn every one night and day with tears.*

This daily activity with tears falls far short in describing Paul's heartfelt burden for his people. No one could ever describe Paul as a weak man. How on earth could he continue his pursuit of lost sinners after all the suffering recorded in 2 Corinthians 11:24-28? As unreal as his lifetime of physical suffering was, it is nothing compared to the spiritual suffering of his broken heart for the lost. Please study and try to grasp the feeling Paul had for his people as given in Romans 9:1-3: *I say the truth in Christ, I lie not, my conscience also bearing me witness in the Holy Ghost, That I have great heaviness and continual sorrow in my heart. For I could wish that myself were accursed from Christ for my brethren, my kinsmen according to the flesh:*

The greatest preacher of all times was a weeping preacher. What kind of reputation did Jesus have as He preached and won souls? *In one circle of the population He was known as "a friend of sinners." To another segment He was known as a powerful, Spirit-filled preacher who reminded them of John the Baptist or the Old Testament prophet Elijah. But in order to reveal that He was a man of tears as He witnessed to individuals personally or preached to a multitude, consider the conversation between Jesus and His disciples in Matthew 16. Jesus asks the apostles the question, *Whom do men say that I the Son of man am?* The apostles began to answer by saying, *Some say that thou art John the Baptist: some, Elias; and others, Jeremias, or one of the prophets* (Matthew 16:13-14).

Why do you think that people were saying that Jesus was Jeremiah? What was Jeremiah noted for? His tears! Jeremiah was known for his burden for his people. When people heard Jesus preach, it reminded them of what they had read and heard about the weeping prophet in the Old Testament, Jeremiah.

Jesus looked at the people He was witnessing to and knew that unless He could win them, they would burn forever in hell.

Jesus prayed to His Father as a good example for men to follow. When He prayed, *it was with strong crying and tears: Who in the days of his flesh, when he had offered up prayers and supplications with strong crying and tears unto him that was able to save him from death, and was heard in that he feared* (Hebrews 5:7).

At a time near the end of His earthly ministry, one can almost hear the sob in the voice of Jesus as He said, *O*

Jerusalem, Jerusalem, thou that killest the prophets, and stonest them which are sent unto thee, how often would I have gathered thy children together, even as a hen gathereth her chickens under her wings, and ye would not! Behold, your house is left unto you desolate (Matthew 23:37-38).

There are no words to describe the love, burden, and compassion of Jesus as He came into this world. The Old Testament prophet Isaiah said He set His face like a flint as He approached His final appointment on the cross. Paul said that in order for Him to become detestable, vulgar sin and die on the cross, separated from His holy Father, he had to set His mind on the finished product in eternity. Jesus looked to, *The joy that was set before Him, endured the cross, despising the shame, and is set down at the right hand of the throne of God* (Hebrews 12:2, emphasis added). The highest, most powerful being, who created and then maintained this vast universe, bowed His head beside a grave one day, and what He did there defies any man to describe the heartbreak, love, and compassion He felt toward His fallen and lost creatures. *Two little words say it all: *Jesus wept.*

The flesh and self-centeredness of man has limited the most powerful weapon man has with God: PRAYER. *What the brethren think and accept has limited man's most powerful weapon in soul winning: TEARS.

Thursday

THE PROMISE OF SUCCESS IN OBEYING THE GREAT COMMISSION

God is not a God who makes obscure promises. It is not difficult to understand God when He made a simple promise to man. Man, because of his spiritual blindness, may not see God's wonderful promise, but it is right there in plain sight for all who want to see.

The promise in keeping the Great Commission and having a successful ministry has the success principle stated not just one time, but twice. These two promises of how to successfully obey the Great Commission and win souls are found in Psalms 126:5-6.

The first promise is addressed to everyone and it states, *They that sow in tears shall reap in joy.* That promise is conditional and if that condition is met, then God promises success: *shall reap in joy* (Psalm 126:5). God broadened that emphatic promise and applied it to a single person in the following verse. He gives the steps for success in soul winning and adds a word to emphasize His promise of success. The word is *doubtless.* He promises that anyone who goes with a burdened heart and weepeth, bearing precious seed (the seed is the Word of God, Matthew 13) shall doubtless come again with his spiritual fruit.

If a person looks at his barren life or ministry, and although there are thousands of sinners all around him, sees just a single sinner here and there get saved, *maybe he should examine his busy schedule, which is not working. Maybe all the things that a modern preacher has been led to believe is "the work of the ministry" is not really the work of the ministry. Maybe he should turn back to his personal life manual, God's Holy Word, which God gave to tune-up his life and prayerfully consider this promise:

The God of heaven who cannot lie and who took an oath upon His honor that He would not lie, promises success.

The incarnate God of heaven, who demonstrated the method of winning souls in His daily life and is a preacher's role model, promises success.

The God of heaven before whom we must all stand and give account of our ministries is the One who promised that if one went out with the Word and sowed in tears, he would win souls.

The God of heaven promised a simple process that leads to success. He promised that he that goeth forth and weepeth, bearing precious seed, shall doubtless come again rejoicing, because souls were saved.

Many men in today's ministry proclaim that soul winning

does not work. *Could it be that the most important aspect, tears, is missing?

*Everything that Jesus did and taught revolves around going out and seeking sinners. It is very clear that as He went, He was not depending upon a mechanical little soul-talk, but He was earnestly striving to save that person from hell.

In one of my training seminars, God drew a lost person to the class on two successive sessions. In the second session, I asked if he would serve as the prospect (sinner) in order for his friend to go through the plan of salvation and win him. He graciously agreed. From a distance I watched the procedure. The friend clearly went through the plan of salvation. He did a thorough and good job explaining the plan of salvation, but the sinner wasn't saved. I went back and got both of their consents for me to go through the same procedure. The young man was gloriously saved. The look on the face of the Christian caused me to ask him, "You are wondering why he got saved when I talked to him but wasn't saved when you had just told him the same message, right?"

My friend said, "Yes."

I said, "Did you go through the plan of salvation just to be going through the plan with him, or did you go through the plan of salvation **to win him?**"

He answered, "Just to go through the plan."

That is exactly what some people are doing, *just going out witnessing, instead of trying to get people saved from hell. I went through the plan in order to win him.

THE CONDITION AND COST OF REVIVAL

Friday

*God is a holy and righteous God who never changes. He is a loving and merciful God who longs to bless His people. He has made many promises that He will honor. In order to get people to trust Him and meet the conditions which will bring His blessings, He established two immutable principles. The word *immutable* means "unchangeable or unalterable." These two immutable principles are (1) God cannot lie, and (2) God took an oath on His own honor that He would not lie.

*There are certain conditions to be met in order for God to bless. These conditions are immutable or unalterable, which means that when a nation or person meets these conditions, whether the nation is Israel or America, God must take action. God not only longs to bless, but He took an oath upon His own honor that He would bless.

God made simple, direct promises to bless and completely turn apostate Israel back to righteousness, as found in Isaiah chapter 58. These same promises apply to our beloved America, if we will only meet the conditions found in Isaiah 58. *These are immutable promises, and the conditions and promised results will not change.

FOUR UNBELIEVABLE PROMISES OF REVIVAL

In order to see these unbelievable promises we will give each verse.

> *Then shall thy light break forth as the morning, and thine health shall spring forth speedily: and thy righteousness shall go before thee; the glory of the LORD shall be thy reward.* (Isaiah 58:8)

> *Then shalt thou call, and the LORD shall answer; thou shalt cry, and he shall say, Here I am.* (Isaiah 58:9)

> *And if thou draw out thy soul to the hungry, and satisfy the afflicted soul; then shall thy light rise in obscurity and thy darkness be as the noon day.* (Isaiah 58:10)

> *Then shalt thou delight thyself in the LORD; and I will cause thee to ride upon the high places of the earth, and feed thee with the heritage of Jacob thy father: for the mouth of the LORD hath spoken it.* (Isaiah 58:14)

Note in verse 8 it states that your light will break forth

as the morning. It will burst forth like the sun coming up in the morning.

In verse 9 God promised to hear their prayer speedily. People will pray and God will bless immediately.

God promises in verse 10 that thy light shall rise from obscurity and be as bright as the noonday sun.

In verse 14 God states that His people would delight themselves in the Lord and ride upon the high places of the earth.

CONDITIONS THAT GOD REQUIRES FOR REVIVAL

Any preacher who desires a nation-changing revival should prayerfully study, pray over, and completely investigate God's standard that He promises to bless in this chapter.

*Again, may we remind the reader that **time does not alter principle**. Anytime people will meet God's requirements, He will respond by doing exceedingly above and beyond man's expectations. But due to time restraints, we list a brief outline of God's standards followed by His promise of blessing.

- **Powerful, Spirit-filled preaching** (verse one): *Cry aloud, spare not, lift up thy voice like a trumpet, and shew my people their transgression* (Isaiah 58:1).

- **In verses 6 and 7 of Isaiah 58, God lists several reasons for** and things to do during periods of fasting.

- **Compassionate consideration to the poor** (verse seven). Among the things God requires is to feed, clothe, shelter, and be a compassionate friend to the poor.

- **Pour out one's soul both in prayer and witnessing** (verse 10). Do not have a judgmental, self-righteous attitude toward the hurting masses (verse 9), *but rather work with them by pouring out your soul (tears), while witnessing and winning them.**

- **Honor the Lord on the Lord's day:** *If thou turn away thy foot from the sabbath, from doing thy pleasure on my holy day; and call the sabbath a delight, the holy of the LORD, honourable; and shalt honour him, not doing thine own ways, nor finding thine own pleasure, nor speaking thine own words* (Isaiah 58:13).

These are five simple requirements which the immutable God of heaven laid down in His Word. If our generation will meet these requirements, our nation will totally change.

GOD'S PROMISES FOR KEEPING AND DOING HIS WORD

These promises were made by God, and only God could bring to pass these marvelous, nation-changing results.

Remember the nature of our merciful God and the price He has already paid in order to demonstrate His great love and power to our beloved nation.

He will again cause the Christian's light to shine brightly (verses 8 and 10). The Christian's light will shine as the brightness of breaking dawn. It will shine as the noonday sun.

God will hear the cries of His people and answer their prayers speedily: *thou shalt cry, and he shall say, Here I am* (Isaiah 58:9).

He will give great Spiritual health which will attract and satisfy seeking souls: *And the LORD shall guide thee continually, and satisfy thy soul in drought, and make fat thy bones: and thou shalt be like a watered garden, and like a spring of water, whose waters fail not* (Isaiah 58:11). God would guide His people continually, satisfy their soul in drought, make their bones fat, and continue to satisfy with fresh, heavenly water.

He will reestablish the glory of the Christian name and the Christian testimony: *And they that shall be of thee shall build the old waste places: thou shalt raise up the foundations of many generations; and thou shalt be called, The repairer of the breach, The restorer of paths* [places] *to dwell* [live] *in* (Isaiah 58:12). He will rebuild the churches, re-establish their message, and repair the foundations. Their testimony would be the repairer of the breach and the restorer of the paths (places) to dwell (live) in.

He will give blessings to the people of our generation that will continue through the millennium (verse 14). He will bless that generation and exalt them with positions of honor in the millennium.

These promises are so great that God had to reaffirm that He would perform them. Note His absolute declaration that finishes this chapter. He said, *for the mouth of the Lord hath spoken it* (Isaiah 58:14).

Summary: Any honest person will have to admit that Jesus and the other successful soul-winners were men who shed tears as they strove to win souls.

There is nothing on this earth that should cause people to weep more that the huge mass of people rushing madly into outer darkness, still lost. Think about it. They will weep forever in hell unless we obey the Great Commission and go out to seek and to save them before it is too late. Christian, it is weep now or weep at the judgment seat and throughout the 1000-year reign.

MONDAY

1. In our society today it is not _____
_____ to use the name of _____.

2. It is _____ incorrect to show any
_____ or especially to shed _____
in religious services.

3. They wept until, *they had no more* _____
to weep (1 Samuel 30:4).

4. This _____ was more like the
_____ of a wounded animal.

5. *Oh my son Absalom, my son, my son Absalom!*
_____ *God* _____ *had died for thee.* (2
Samuel 18:33)

TUESDAY

1. He said that he _____ his couch with
_____.

2. *They that* _____ [the Word] *in tears shall*
_____ *in joy* (Psalms 126:5).

3. A broken and _____ heart is a
heart which _____ tears.

4. He was known as the _____
prophet and was _____ and greatly persecuted
by his countrymen.

5. *That I might weep* _____ *and* _____
for the slain of the daughter of my people (Jeremiah 9:1).

WEDNESDAY

1. *That by the space of _____ years I _____*
not to warn every one day and night with tears (Acts 20:31).

2. In one circle of the _____ He
was known as "a _____ of sinners."

3. It was with "_____ crying and _____."

4. Two little words say it all: _____ _____.

5. What the brethren think and accept has
_____ man's most powerful weapon in
soul winning: _____.

THURSDAY

1. *They that sow in _____ shall reap in _____.*

2. Maybe he should _____ his
busy _____, which is not working.

3. Could it be that the most important
_____, tears, that make soul winning
work, is _____?

4. Everything that Jesus did and _____
revolves around going out and _____
sinners.

5. Just going out _____ instead of
trying to get people _____ from _____.

FRIDAY

1. God is a _____ and _____
God who never changes.

2. There are certain _____ to be
met in order for God to _____.

3. These are _____ promises and
the conditions and promised _____
_____ _____ _____.

4. Again, may we remind the reader that
_____ _____ _____ ALTER
_____.

5. But rather _____ with them by pouring out
your _____ (tears), while witnessing and winning them.

DAILY DECLARATION

Lesson Eleven

Repeat Aloud Each Morning and Evening

Many people in Jesus' day thought he was the prophet Jeremiah, because Jesus wept as he preached and won souls.

MEMORY VERSE:

He that goeth forth and weepeth, bearing precious seed, shall doubtless come again with rejoicing, bringing his sheaves with him. (Psalm 126:6)

CHECK BLOCK AFTER REPEATING

	Mon	Tues	Wed	Thurs	Fri	Sat	Sun
A.M.							
P.M.							

My daily prayer to God will be: Lord, touch my hard heart and my unbelief so I will learn to weep over the lost.

_____

Name   Grade

LESSON TWELVE

GOD'S GIFT TO PASTORS FOR OBEYING THE GREAT COMMISSION

Monday

PART ONE

A SIMPLE PLAN FOR SELF-MOTIVATION

We have two headings for this final lesson. *"God's Gift to Pastors" and "A Simple Plan for Self-Motivation." Both statements mean the same thing. The preachers have a position similar to the quarterback on a football team. *The football team that has a good quarterback wins most of their games. Dr. Lee Robertson would always say, *"Everything rises and falls on leadership." This is absolutely true concerning the success and growth in a local church.

*Much of the pastor's job is in the realm of motivation. From his pulpit-preaching to the individual counseling he does, the end goal is to instill new hope and zeal within the believer. I heard a story about a successful pastor who was considered eccentric by some of his members. Every day at noon the pastor stopped whatever he was doing, got into his car, and raced across town to the railroad station. He would generally sit in his car for a few minutes and then return to his church as pastor. People began to talk about it, and the deacons took it upon themselves to confront the pastor about his peculiar behavior. The pastor's answer to the deacons illustrates my point. He said, "Nothing in this church succeeds unless I push it. There is only one thing in the whole area that goes without me pushing it – the train, which comes through our town every day at noon. I don't have to push that train. If you stop me from going down and watching that train every day, then I am out of here. You have my resignation." In most local churches *everything rises and falls upon the preacher's motivation and leadership.

Tuesday

WHO MOTIVATES THE PREACHER?

*But the question arises, "Who motivates the preacher?" God is the only one who knows what confronts the pastor each week. Sometimes it is something every hour: the death of a key member, hostility from a backslidden person, a broken home and marriage that he could not repair or, it may lie within his own family, where sickness or financial pressures exist. Bear in mind, the opposing team is concentrating on stopping the quarterback. The captain of the opposing team, *the Devil, is concentrating on stopping or hindering the pastor. So the question arises, "Who motivates or encourages the pastor?" *The church will become less successful if the pressures of life cause the pastor to become discouraged. Many good men who failed to have encouragement began to wear down and say, "What's the use?" or "It is not worth it" and quit the ministry. It is to these men and to every preacher that we present a simple plan of self-motivation. This plan will apply to and help all believers, but it is especially true for pastors. Consider God's gift to pastors: There are three different Scriptures which reveal this key for self-motivation. These Scriptures, given by the Lord to the apostles, transformed them *from unmotivated men into men who could not be stopped and who became the most successful leaders in the history of the church. *This motivation comes in the form of positions which are offered to preachers in the future world. Abraham went from being uncertain Abram to being the friend-of-God Abraham, because he looked for a city that had foundations. Notice the word *foundations* – plural – which was the New Jerusalem. Moses refused the throne of the world's most powerful nation because he *Had respect unto the recompense of the rewards ... seeing Him who is invisible* (Hebrews 11:26-27).

Wednesday

THE BROAD VIEW OF A PREACHER'S FUTURE

We will try to give the preachers a broad vision of God's will for their eternal welfare in this section.

BUG'S-EYE OR BIRD'S-EYE VIEW?

Over fifty years ago when I was in Bible college, we would have different speakers in to preach Chapel. One of the favorite Chapel speakers was Dr. Corbet Maak. He was a powerful speaker who always challenged the students. One of his main themes was **"Do you have a bug's-eye or a bird's-eye vision?"** He went on and explained what the difference was between a bug's-eye and bird's-eye view. A bug lives on the ground and is surrounded by weeds and grass. A small rise in the ground looks like a mountain to him. *A bird can sit in the top of the tallest tree or soar far up into the sky, where it has a limitless view of the beauty of God's creation. A bug's-eye view is limited, so the poor little bug can't see the vastness of God's creation and beauty. The bird's-eye view is vast and unrestricted; he can see the beauty and the actions of the creatures around him. *A bug's-eye view is earthly, while the bird's-eye view is heavenly. *A bug's-eye view was limited, while a bird's-eye view could see beyond the horizon. The bug's-eye view in a preacher's life is seeing the horrible, scary things going on in the world (weeds and tall grass), *while the preachers who have the bird's-eye view are looking beyond this earthly life (earthly horizon) and seeing the great promises and adventures that are waiting to be experienced in the coming millennial reign and on into the eternal age. Ephesians 2:6-7 talks about this bird's-eye view that Paul had. *He said it would take ages for God to show what He had in store for His faithful men who obeyed the Great Commission. *And hath raised us up together, and made us sit together in heavenly places in Christ Jesus: That in the ages to come he might shew the exceeding riches of his grace in his kindness toward us through Christ Jesus* (Eph. 2:6-7).

Thursday

PREACHER, GOD OFFERS YOU A POSITION TO SHARE HIS AUTHORITY AND HIS GLORY

Our sub-heading is absolutely true! Jesus offers you a position to share His authority and glory, BUT YOU HAVE TO EARN IT!

The way you can earn it is through sacrifice – hard, long hours and possible suffering. You won't earn it through your becoming smile, pleasant personality, or even your standing with your preacher brethren.

He is not impressed by those virtues. *This wonderful position will be rewarded by how you obey the Great Commission in training a work-force in order to attempt to save poor sinners from hell. *But think about your paycheck! If you submit to Him as your sole Lord and boss and complete the task and purpose of your ministry, *He promises that you can share in His authority over this earth for 1000 years. *He even broadens that promise and promises you an opportunity to share in His eternal glory through the vast eternal ages. Wow! That boggles the human mind. It is unbelievable that the God of all creation and the One who controls the movements of all earthly creatures as well as the vast movement of the galaxies offers to you, a poor, frail human being, the opportunity to share in His authority and in His eternal glory. What can I say? Unbelievable, but it is true!

Share His authority throughout the coming 1000-year reign. The Bible absolutely promises that Jesus is coming back to this earth as a king. He will sit on David's throne in the city of Jerusalem and rule over this world as the second Adam for 1000 years. The curse will be taken off of the earth, and the nature of all animals will cause them to dwell together in peace. *The earth will be full of the knowledge of the Lord as the waters cover the sea. *They shall not hurt nor destroy in all my holy* *mountain: for the earth shall be full of the knowledge of the LORD, as the waters cover the sea* (Isaiah 11:9).

Friday

REWARDS FOR OBEYING THE GREAT COMMISSION

*God promises great rewards to those who give their lives fully to obey the Great Commission. The Great Commission commands people to live their lives in an effort to get the gospel to every creature alive on earth in their generation. Note the word *fully* – those who give their lives fully, not just attend a church and be a part-time Christian, but work at being an obedient Christian every day of his life. *It is to this type of person that the promise is made. In the marvelous promises which Jesus made to the overcomers in the seven churches recorded in Revelation, we have this wonderful promise. Please note the clearly stated promises to His children who were overcomers in the Thyatira church. There was a lot of confusion and false doctrine in and around Thyatira. It was not easy to live the Christian life there. That may be the reason Jesus made this emphatic promise: *And he that overcometh, and keepeth my works unto the end, to him will I give power over the nations* (Revelation 2:26).

The statement *to him will I give power over the nations* is very clear and easy to understand. The word *power* means "authority," and the authority is to share in ruling with Christ for 1000 years. A person who makes Jesus his Lord and works to fulfill the Great Commission of preaching the gospel to every creature until the rapture or the end of his life is a candidate for sharing in Jesus' authority during the coming 1000-year reign.

A stronger promise of actually sharing in Jesus' authority is made to the overcomers in the Laodicean Church; *To him that overcometh will I grant to sit with me in my throne, even as I also overcame, and am set down with my Father in his throne* (Revelation 3:21).

If a person can take the promises of God at face value, then it should be clear to him that the statement *sit with me on my throne* means share his authority over the nations. I am sure that within someone's mind the question arises, "How does one overcome, and what does he have to overcome?" The answer to that question is found in 1 John 5:4; *For whatsoever is born of God overcometh the world: and this is the victory that overcometh the world, even our faith.*

*We overcome by obeying the commands of God by faith. We look to Him. By faith we keep our focus on Jesus, His Word, and the promises He made. The just or saved are to walk or live by faith.

The question of what one has to overcome in order to be an overcomer is found in the parable of the sower as recorded in Matthew 13, Mark 4, and Luke 8. Matthew declares what a believer must overcome as the cares of this world and the deceitfulness of riches. In Mark 4:19, Mark adds *and the lusts of other things* to the two which Matthew gave. Dr. Luke adds another item to the list which Matthew and Mark gave. This major obstacle to overcome is revealed as *the pleasures of life* (Luke 8:14). The preachers who worry about Obama, the economy, and what is in their retirement fund probably have a bug's-eye view.

Many pastors are really concerned about the lust of other things, meaning gaining complete power in a local church or having their own way in matters pertaining to their interests. The pleasures of this life mean that there is a temptation for leisure and soft living instead of enduring hardness as a soldier of Jesus Christ. Oh, the poor preachers who are falling victim to the cares of this life, deceitfulness of riches, the lust of other things, and the pleasure of life will find at the judgment seat that they did so at the expense of sharing Christ's authority and eternal glory. Their unbelief disqualified them. They traded the big house on this earth for a shack in the millennium.

Oh, dear brother, look again. Give everything you have now in obeying the Great Commission, claiming His promise that was made to you to share in His authority for 1000 years, and then in sharing Jesus' eternal glory forever.

The promise of sharing in Jesus' eternal glory. The fifth chapter of 1 Peter is written primarily to preachers. In the first eleven verses the word *glory*, is found four times.

In verse one we have the statement made to pastors, *A partaker of the glory that shall be revealed.*

In verse four we have the promise, *When the chief Shepherd shall appear* [second coming], *ye shall receive a crown of glory that fadeth not away.*

In verse ten we have the statement, **The God of all grace, who hath called us unto His eternal glory by Christ Jesus.*

In verse eleven Peter gives worthy praise to Jesus, *To him* [Jesus] *be glory and dominion for ever and ever. Amen.*

Notice the teaching of these verses which was given to preachers. Verse one states that a preacher, if he qualifies by working as he should, can earn a crown of glory.

Verse four states that the crown of glory will never fade, for it will shine brightly forever.

Verse ten makes clear what the purpose a call into the ministry is and with whom and what level the glory will be. It is to share the glory of Jesus, and it will be forever.

In verse eleven we have God pinpointing who is

responsible for our opportunity to share His glory and dominion. It is unto Jesus, and He made the emphatic statement of how long we will share His glory and leadership. It is not forever. It is not even forever and forever. Both of these statements are true, but because the promise is so awesome, the inspired writer was moved to say, *for ever and ever. Amen.* The "amen" there is God's way of emphasizing that truth.

MONDAY

1. "God's _____ to Pastors" and "A _____ Plan for Self-Motivation."

2. The _____ team that has a good _____ wins most of their games.

3. "Everything _____ and _____ on leadership."

4. Much of the pastor's job is in the _____ of _____.

5. Everything rises and falls upon the _____ motivation and _____.

TUESDAY

1. But the question arises, "_____ motivates the _____?"

2. The Devil is _____ on stopping or _____ the pastor.

3. The church will become _____ successful if the _____ of life cause the pastor to become _____.

4. From _____ men into men who could not be _____.

5. This motivation comes in the form of
_____ which are offered to preachers in the _____ world.

WEDNESDAY

1. A _____ can sit in the top of the
_____ tree or soar far up into the sky,
where it has a _____ view.

2. A _____-eye view is earthly, while the
_____-eye view is heavenly.

3. A bug's-eye view was _____,
while a bird's-eye view could see beyond the
_____.

4. While the preachers who have the _____
_____ _____ are looking beyond
this earthly life,

5. He said it would take _____ for God to show
what He had in store for His _____
men.

THURSDAY

1. This wonderful _____ will
be rewarded by how you _____ the Great
Commission.

2. But _____ about your _____!

3. He _____ that you can share in His
_____ over this earth for 1000 years.

4. He even broadens that promise and promises
you an _____ to share in His
_____ glory.

5. The earth will be full of the _____
of the Lord as the _____ cover the sea.

FRIDAY

1. God promises _____ rewards to those
who give their lives _____ to obey the
Great Commission.

2. It is to this _____ of person that the
_____ is made.

3. *Sit with me on my* _____ means
share my _____ over the nations.

4. We _____ by obeying the commands of God by _____.

5. *The God of all* _____, *who hath*
_____ *us unto His eternal glory.*

DAILY DECLARATION

Lesson Twelve

Repeat Aloud Each Morning and Evening

Jesus promises that I can share in his eternal glory if I will give myself to obeying the Great Commission.

MEMORY VERSE:

But the God of all grace, who hath called us unto his eternal glory by Christ Jesus, after that ye have suffered a while, make you perfect, stablish, strengthen, settle you. (1 Peter 5:10)

CHECK BLOCK AFTER REPEATING

	Mon	Tues	Wed	Thurs	Fri	Sat	Sun
A.M.							
P.M.							

I will give myself to work for things which are eternal, since I am an eternal being.

Name   Grade

LESSON THIRTEEN

GOD'S GIFT TO PASTORS WHO LEAD IN OBEYING THE GREAT COMMISSION

Monday

PART TWO

A SIMPLE PLAN FOR SELF-MOTIVATION

Why does the formula work? It is in harmony with man's nature.

*This formula completely transformed the unmotivated apostles into men who could not be stopped.

Why is the formula so successful?

It gets man's mind off himself.

It gets man's mind off what the brethren think.

It gets man's mind off his problems.

It gets man's mind off the world.

What is this marvelous formula?

This marvelous formula that transformed the apostles and will transform today is found in three words.

Those three words are: *Seek, Pray,* and *Look.*

One of Jesus' first commandments to the apostles was to **seek first** the kingdom of God (Matthew 6:33).

The Lord later taught the apostles to **pray daily** for the kingdom to come.

The final ingredient in the formula was to **look for His kingdom** (Titus 2:13).

Having problems and don't know what to do? Seek first the kingdom of God and His righteousness (will).

Having a hard time with meager results, maybe in prison or suffering physical problems? Lift up your heart and pray for His kingdom to come. *Look to your future place of eternal glory. Remember, if you suffer with Him, you will reign with Him.

Need a fresh anointing of your purpose and calling? Let the grace of God teach you once again to look for His glorious appearing. Remember John 3:12.

*Place these three words into your mind: ***Seek, Pray,*** and ***Look.***

*Place these three words into your subconscious mind: ***Seek, Pray, Look.***

*Keep on using the three major words that transformed the early Christians until they transform you.

Seek first the kingdom.

Pray daily for His kingdom.

Look constantly for His kingdom.

Tuesday

THE FIRST STEP TO BUILDING SELF-MOTIVATION

The first step in self-motivation is a step that few preachers ever learn. It is a step God continually uses in helping believers. When stressing an important point, the wording or something similar in wording is repeated over and over again throughout the Bible. For example, the Scripture states in several places, *the just shall walk by faith* (Galatians 3:14). It is by faith that elders (preachers) earn a good report (Hebrews 11:2).

The first lesson Jesus gave to the apostles had to do with their primary purpose. He told Peter, Andrew, John, and James to follow Him, and He would make them fishers of men. Luke spoke more directly and said, *Henceforth you will catch men.* *These statements prove that the primary purpose of each believer is to win souls. In order for them to learn that new vocation and be successful in fulfilling God's purpose and will for their lives, they had to learn to trust God.

When the apostles were still in training as new converts,

Jesus gave them a conditional promise. It is in the conditional promise that we have the first word that will help the preacher learn to be self-motivated. It is the word *seek*! The word **seek** is found in Matthew 6:33: *But seek ye first the kingdom of God, and his righteousness; and all these things shall be added unto you.*

Notice the awesome promise made to these preachers in training. The promise is made personally by Jesus to His first disciples. *He promises that He will personally supply everything they need to be successful workers if they seek first the kingdom of God and His righteous will for their lives. Earlier in the chapter, He stated that He fed the birds and clothed the flowers. In fact, *it is God's good pleasure to supply every need that any of His children have. But the condition of taking care of all of their needs was based on their seeking the kingdom of God and His righteous will for their lives. One can capture that promise by placing the word **seek** into his mind and soul. Seek first His kingdom's work and His righteous will, and He will take care of and supply all of one's needs. He may have to use a raven as He did with Elijah, but since He is Lord of all birds, He can do that.

He then began to build the faith of His disciples by feeding 5000 men with a few fishes and bread. He showed His great power one night when *He commanded the waves to *be still*, and calmed the sea. He showed His mighty faith-building power by raising the dead. These first preachers were commanded to seek first the king-dom of God and His righteous will for their lives, and He would fully take care of them and their needs. That same promise is made to you, preacher, by the immu-table God of heaven who cannot lie and who took an oath on His own honor that He would not lie. The one word to get into your mind in order to motivate your-self regardless of any stress, problem, or circumstance is the word *SEEK*!

My testimony is that God has honored His promise for over sixty-five years in supplying my every need. The reason? Because I have obeyed and practiced His com-mand to *seek first His kingdom.*

Wednesday

THE NEXT WORD IN SELF-MOTIVATION IS PRAY

The second word in learning the secret of self-motivation is *PRAY.* In the eleventh chapter of Luke we have the apostles coming upon Jesus while Jesus was praying. When he finished praying, the apostles asked Jesus, *Lord, teach us to pray, as John also taught his disciples* to pray (Luke 11:1). *Jesus answered their request by giving the apostles a command. He said, *When ye pray, say.* That is not a suggestion on the part of Jesus, but a command. *When* ye *pray, say!* Jesus then gave them a model to follow as they prayed every day. You ask, "How do you know they were commanded to pray the model prayer every day?" I know because the third thing on the daily prayer list was the command to ask for their daily bread. How could one ask for their daily bread if they did not pray every day?

Notice that after they were to come humbly before God and address the great God of the universe as their father, He gave them a prayer list to follow. *The first thing on the prayer list was about the coming kingdom. The second thing on their prayer list was concerning God's will for their lives. The third thing was for their daily provisions, and so on. For a complete commentary on the model prayer, order the author's book, **Grandpa, Teach Me to Pray.**

PREACHER, LEARN THIS FACT!

*God is attempting to work everything that happens to you for your eternal good. You are called to share His eternal glory. Loving parents' goals are not to work only for the success of their little child's benefit in kindergarten. Their goal is to train their child, so the child can live a successful, rewarding life. They are very concerned about their child in kindergarten, but kindergarten is one of the first steps they guide him through so he can live successfully for a lifetime. This life is your kindergarten phase of life. Some of the things that seem bad may happen in kindergarten (this lifetime), but are designed by God for your eternal good. Notice this truth which is stated in 2 Corinthians 4:17, *For our light affliction, which is but for a moment, worketh for us a far more exceeding and eternal weight of glory.*

The afflictions (troubles, problems) which last but for a moment (compared to the eternal ages) worketh or are designed for our eternal good. So Jesus gave the model prayer for our eternal good. It is a prayer that is designed to lift one's mind off his problems and difficulties and focus on the coming 1000-year reign. The Christian is to pray, *Thy kingdom come.* *This prayer will also serve to get his mind off the cares of this perishing world. It will help him to not fall into the pit that is dug by the deceitfulness of riches or the lust of other things. He will not be as likely to squander his positions of ruling and reigning with Christ for 1000 years by pursuing the pleasures of life for a short season. John Wesley and George Whitefield taught their converts to pray the model prayer every day. *Praying the model prayer every day had a tremendous effect in fanning the fires of revival in the first great spiritual awakening that started in 1734.

THE REAL PURPOSE FOR PRAYING "THY KINGDOM COME"

Thursday

A person may wonder, "What is the purpose or benefit for praying, 'Thy kingdom come' every day?" In order to fully appreciate the purpose and benefit for praying the model prayer every day, one must understand the reason the commandment was given.

THE SPIRITUAL CONDITIONS OF THE APOSTLES

We often look up to the apostles as superstars, and well, we should. But a close investigation into their lives shows that most of the apostles had periods of difficulty in their spiritual growth. *There were periods where they were scared, faithless, and unmotivated.

Something had to help them endure the tremendous pressure they felt as everyone in Jerusalem was talking about the Jewish leaders who had decided to capture Jesus, give Him a mock trial, and then crucify Him. All of the apostles knew of the plot, and they thought their world and ministry would end when it happened. They had given their full time and energy in following Jesus and wondered what would happen to them when Jesus was crucified. *They also wanted to know what they would receive for their services. As unspiritual as this may seem, the apostles, through Peter, asked Jesus what they would be paid or rewarded for fully giving themselves in following Jesus. When Peter asked these questions, Jesus calmly answered, *And I appoint unto you a kingdom, as my Father hath appointed unto me; That ye may eat and drink at my table in my kingdom, and sit on thrones judging the twelve tribes of Israel* (Luke 22:29-30).

THEIR REWARD WAS TWO-FOLD

*First, they each would become a king who would sit on a throne over one of the twelve tribes of Israel. Think about it! From being a hard-working, common man working as a commercial fisherman to a palace, where he would sit on a throne as a king for 1000 years.

*Second, he would have a regular place at the dinner table of the King of Kings and Lord of Lords for a full 1000 years. When Abraham, Daniel, or Elijah would come into town, the apostles would entertain and fellowship with them.

Do you see why Jesus taught these men to pray *Thy kingdom come* every day? *It was to keep in their minds the great promise of ruling and reigning with Christ for 1000 years. The Devil and the world could not stop them. They would simply pray *Thy kingdom come*. Oh, praise the Lord! If He came today, I would get my throne for 1000 years. I would get my place at Jesus' table for 1000 years. If they kill me, praise the Lord! I will have my seat at Jesus' table. If I suffer with Him, I will reign with Him. If I get killed while obeying Him to get the gospel to every creature in the entire world, I will get the martyr's crown. Jesus is working all things together for my eternal good. This light affliction will increase my eternal rewards. Preacher, the key word here to get into your mind is *PRAY!*

Seek, Pray, and our final word for self-motivation is ***Look***.

Seek the Kingdom,

Pray for the Kingdom to come, and

Look for the Kingdom.

Friday

V. THE FINAL WORD IN SELF-MOTIVATION IS LOOK

*On the night before Jesus was crucified, He told His disciples about His second coming. He said, *And if I go and prepare a place for you, **I will come again**, and receive you unto myself; that where I am, there ye may be also. And whither I go ye know, and the way ye know* (John 14:3-4, emphasis added).

Forty days later as the disciples stared up in the sky

and watched His ascension back into heaven, angels appeared and said, *And while they looked stedfastly toward heaven as he went up, behold, two men stood by them in white apparel; Which also said, Ye men of Galilee, why stand ye gazing up into heaven?* *__this same Jesus, which is taken up from you__ into heaven, shall so come in like manner as ye have seen him go into heaven* (Acts 1:10-11, emphasis added).

*Jesus had recently taught the disciples on the mount about His second coming. During His message He said, *Be ye therefore ready also: for the Son of man cometh at an hour when ye think not* (Luke 12:40).

With all of these statements about His coming, *the disciples were looking for Jesus to come back at any time. They reasoned that since Jesus had created the whole world and everything in it in six days, then building a few little old mansions was nothing. He may be back today.

This belief fanned the fires of zeal and purity. 1 John 3:2-3 reveals that the belief in the imminent return of Christ would cause a believer to purify himself: *Beloved, now are we the sons of God, and it doth not yet appear what we shall be: but we know that, when he shall appear, we shall be like him; for we shall see him as he is. And every man that hath this hope in him purifieth himself, even as he is pure.*

Titus 2:11-14 teaches that looking for the second coming would produce holy and zealous living. *The key word for self-motivation is *Looking* for the blessed hope and glorious appearing. *For the grace of God that bringeth salvation hath appeared to all men, Teaching us that, denying ungodliness and worldly lusts, we should live soberly, righteously, and godly, in this present world;* **Looking for that blessed hope,** *and the glorious appearing of the great God and our Saviour Jesus Christ; Who gave himself for us, that he might redeem us from all iniquity, and purify unto himself a peculiar people, zealous of good works* (Titus 2:11-14, emphasis added).

If a person will **Seek** first the kingdom,

If a person will **Pray** for the kingdom,

If a person will **Look** for the kingdom,

They will have a powerful life which **will give them a good hair day at the judgment seat of Christ**. They will hear Jesus say, "Well done" and be appointed an area somewhere on this earth to govern for 1000 years.

Seek first the kingdom!

Pray for the kingdom!

Look for the kingdom every day in this short life and live in a big house and reign with Christ over this earth for 1000 years!

MONDAY

1. This formula _____ transformed the unmotivated apostles into men who could not be _____.

2. Look to your _____ place of _____ glory.

3. Place these words into your mind: _____, _____, and _____.

4. Place these three words into your _____ _____; *Seek, Pray, Look.*

5. Keep on using the three _____ words which transformed the _____ Christians until they transform _____.

TUESDAY

1. *The _____ shall _____ by faith.*

2. These statements prove that the _____ purpose of each believer is to _____ _____.

3. He promises that He will _____ supply _____ they need to be successful workers.

4. It is God's good _____ to supply
every _____ that any of His children have.

5. He commanded the waves to *be* _____,
and _____ the sea.

WEDNESDAY

1. Jesus answered their request by giving the apostles
a _____. He said, *When ye*
_____, _____.

2. The _____ thing on the prayer list was about
the _____ kingdom.

3. God is attempting to work everything that
_____ to you for your
_____ _____.

4. This prayer will also serve to get his mind _____
the cares of this _____ world.

5. Praying the _____ prayer every day
had a _____, effect.

THURSDAY

1. There were periods where they
were _____,
_____ and unmotivated.

2. They also wanted to know what they would
_____ for their _____.

3. **First,** they would become a _____ who
would sit on a throne over one of the _____
tribes of Israel.

4. **Second,** he would have a _____ place
at the _____ table of the King of Kings.

5. It was to keep in their _____ the great
promise of_____ and_____
with Christ for 1000 years.

FRIDAY

1. On the night before Jesus was _____,
He told His disciples about His _____
_____.

2. *This same Jesus which is _____ _____*
from you into heaven, shall so come in _____
manner (Acts 1:10-11).

3. Jesus had recently _____ the disciples on the mount about His _____
_____.

4. The _____ were
_____ for Jesus to come back at any
time.

5. The key word for _____ _____
is _____ for the blessed hope and
glorious appearing.

DAILY DECLARATION

Lesson Thirteen

Repeat Aloud Each Morning and Evening

God wants me to live a positive life of faith so He can do great things through me.

MEMORY VERSE:

But seek ye first the kingdom of God, and his righteousness; and all these things shall be added unto you. (Matthew 6:33)

CHECK BLOCK AFTER REPEATING

	Mon	Tues	Wed	Thurs	Fri	Sat	Sun
A.M.							
P.M.							

I will obey His commands to seek first His kingdom, to pray daily for His kingdom, and look continually for His kingdom.

Name   **Grade**

Be All That You Can Be By the Grace of God

God placed you on the earth for a purpose. How you fulfill that purpose will direct where and how you will live in the 1000-year reign on this earth and throughout eternity.

When a person is born again, he receives a new vocation or job. He no longer is boss of his life. He yielded that right when he received Jesus as his Saviour. His new vocation under the Great Commission is to keep people from suffering in hell by telling them about God's love and plan for their lives.

Everything that is healthy reproduces after its kind; cattle after their kind and marriages produce children (after their kind). This principle is true in the spiritual realm also. The Bible declares that the fruit (by-product) of the righteous (saved) is a tree of life (producing life to others), and he that winneth souls is wise.

The Christian's new vocation is winning souls.

This book not only reveals your new vocation as a Christian, but enables you to overcome your fear and to able to confidently share your faith with your family and friends.

Salt Lake Bible College

FREE and Accredited

www.saltlakebiblecollege.org

Contact Dr. T.E. VanBuskirk

docvbk@saltlakebiblecollege.org

ABOUT THE AUTHOR

Dr. James Wilkins is an author, teacher, pastor, evangelist, and director of New Testament Ministries. Dr. Wilkins has been privileged with starting thirteen churches. He has taught in several Independent Baptist Bible colleges, authored more than sixty books and booklets, spoken on national TV and radio, and has preached over 44,000 times.

Dr. Wilkins' heart and soul has always been in the area of soul winning and discipleship. And with books like *The Drama at the Cross, Designed to Win,* and *The Milk of the Word,* he has been not only seeing souls saved, but has also been building a lasting foundation for faith.

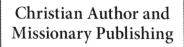

ADDITIONAL BOOKS AVAILABLE FROM NEW TESTAMENT MINISTRIES

Soul-Winning Books

Perfecting the Saints

Perfecting the Saints is a command to evangelists, pastors, and teachers. This book will help believers grow so they can do "the work of the ministry." It will help them develop in the following areas:

- Walking by faith

- Overcoming visitation fright and insecurities

- Recognizing and overcoming the Devil's attacks

- Overcoming their awkwardness in witnessing

Perfecting the Saints is a textbook used in the first hour of the Personal Growth Seminar, which is a five-week course developed by the author, who has gone soul winning each week for over sixty years.

Designed to Win

Everything was designed by its Creator to reproduce. *And God said; Let the earth bring forth the living creature after his kind* (Genesis 1:24).

Christianity has become a mere philosophy in this nominal twenty-first century. A person is considered a good Christian if he lives a separated life and believes in the fundamentals of the faith. But Jesus said, *Herein is my Father glorified, that ye bear much fruit.*

YOU BEAR MUCH FRUIT by winning many souls. Then He goes ahead and refers to a principle which is accepted by mankind throughout the world. When a tree produces large, well-formed, delicious fruit in abundance, it is recognized as a good tree. He said, so shall ye be (made manifest) my disciples; that is, when you win many souls (much fruit), you manifest yourself to those watching as a good Christian and your heavenly Father is glorified.

This book, *Designed to Win*, is written on the premise that if all saved people are to bear fruit or win souls, then the process of soul winning has to be simple! If all are to do it, if all can do it, soul winning must be simple!

Observe To Do

In the sixth chapter of Acts the apostles asked the church for help so they could give themselves continually to prayer and to the ministry of the Word. This request was not in order for them to go into their studies and prepare the message they were  to preach. It was to minister the Word in giving on-the-job training from house to house as they developed their members to do the work of the ministry.

Paul was totally committed to show and teach them principles in soul winning and discipleship publicly and from house to house (Acts 20:20).

We must return to the Bible pattern of teaching our members to OBSERVE TO DO instead of just teaching the Word.

Discipleship Books

The Milk of the Word

The Milk of the Word is a self-help book that will equip the reader to be discipled and take what he has learned and disciple others.

The Milk of the Word teaches not only how to know God's Word but also how to do God's Word.

The Milk of the Word is part one of the *New Convert Care* program, which teaches how to follow up, protect, and develop new Christians.

From Salvation to Service

This booklet is designed to be given to the new convert the moment he is saved. It explains the salvation process and teaches him to beware of his adversaries, the Devil, and the flesh.

Questions Concerning Baptism

This book answers some of the most confusing questions about biblical baptism and is designed to be given to those who have been saved but are unsure of baptism. What is baptism? How should baptism be performed and when? Should I be baptized again? What's the purpose of baptism? This book is also an excellent source of information about proper biblical baptism and has taught many people of their need to be scripturally baptized.

Doctrinal Books

Meat of the Word

This is book three in the *New Convert* series. This book is designed to put spiritual truths into the heart of the Christian that will cause him to grow in faith. Some of the chapter titles are: God's Course for His Children, God's Comforter for His Children, God's Crowns for His Children, and God's Coming for His Children.

The Other Side of the River (1,000-Year Reign of Christ)

With the second coming of Christ looming ever nearer, it is time for us to consider what our address will be "across the river" in the Millennium.

This book will give you a clearer view of the one thousand years of peace on this earth before we go into our eternal abode.

How you serve Jesus NOW will dictate what your address will be for a full thousand years. WILL you live as a king or as a pauper?

Books for Hurting People

Healing Words For Hurting People

A young man at the height of his success with everything in his life going right suddenly screams out, *I was greatly afflicted* and *All men are liars.* As David was living his dream, he woke up one morning and suddenly his dream turned into a nightmare. Within a few short days the person he loved and admired tried to murder him. He became a fugitive with a price on his head, most of his friends forsook him, his darling wife left him for another man, and he was hungry and alone with no place to go.

How did David, a young man in his twenties, overcome these heartbreaking experiences to walk and live a victorious life? You owe it to yourself to hear his testimony of how he rose from the depths of despair to become Israel's greatest king. This book holds the secret of being set free so one can live again. This book contains more than a few principles that will help a person; it is a road map to a life of victory.

Healing Words for Addicted People

This book was written for anyone who is fighting a losing battle.

ESPECIALLY …

To those who are struggling with addictions! God's Word promises absolute victory IF and when one follows truths that lift them from defeat to victorious living.

Truth One – The Proper Recognition – God

Truth Two – The Proper Manual – The Bible

Truth Three – The Proper Lifestyle – I'm the Lord's

Truth Four – The Proper Protection – The Church

In a world of no hope, there is hope and victory … and it is for you, the addict, and the struggling Christian.

The dog you feed – CONTROLS!

Healing Words for Lonely People

Healing Words for Lonely People comes from the heart of a pastor who has over fifty years of experience comforting bereaved or lonely people. In fact, his life was redirected as a result of the sudden death of his brother Wayne.

Dr. Wilkins has a vivid memory of the pain and confusion he experienced when he received the news of the accidental death of his brother. Less than a year later his father unexpectedly died, which caused him to turn to *the Father of mercies, and the God of all comfort*(2 Corinthians 1:3).

As a pastor he has aided countless families in their hours of sorrow. As a man, one can imagine his personal pain by reading the dedication page as found in the front of this booklet. This book also offers scientific data that will help control loneliness.

Healing Words for Lonely People could be a treasured gift to both those who are suffering and the friends who comfort them.

A Baby's Viewpoint of Life and Death

A child dies for three hours, lives in heaven, and then returns. Wouldn't you expect her to have a message?

She will teach you about heaven and other important issues of life.

Her message will help and comfort those who have lost a child or loved one.

Her life blessed everyone she came in contact with and it will enrich those who read *A Baby's Viewpoint of Life and Death*.

Books for Teenagers

A Preacher Boy's Little Faith

This is a story of God's wondrous grace in the life of a struggling young preacher.

This transparent story is of one young man's determination to keep his end of the covenant he made with his God. This book will strengthen the faith of all who read it.

This true story covers the first four years of Dr. James Wilkins' sixty years in the ministry.

The Healing of a Rebel

Bitterness, unforgiveness, and hatred affect more people, and are oftentimes more destructive than cancer.

Through the story of a boy who had been rejected by his parents and wounded by religion, Dr. Wilkins dramatically shows the only cure for these "diseases" which plague the human race.

The adventure begins with a car chase and ends with a transformed young man giving his life in service to God.

The story revolves around a rebellious high school sports star, a wise pastor, and his beautiful, athletic daughter. *The Healing of a Rebel* will educate, entertain, and help multitudes find lasting peace and happiness.

Books of Inspiration

Lasting Moments of Joy Series

These are soul-winning experiences that happened throughout my lifetime but will produce eternal joy. The following stories happened – in a moment of time.

More Lasting Moments of Joy

Stories for dog lovers

Stories for travelers

One story entitled "Is my baby in hell?"

Another story about the conversion of a Muslim

Stories of the helpless and hopeless who found peace

Stories which both the religious and non-religious will enjoy

Favorite Lasting Moments of Joy

The latest volume, *Favorite Lasting Moments of Joy*, is a book about some of the people who have made the greatest investment in my life and ministry. This book is also designed to help young parents build a desire into their children to develop a lifestyle of soul winning.

Books that Increase Regular and Faith-Promise Giving

Dr. Wilkins has been a church planter (thirteen churches), a missionary-minded pastor, and has taught missions courses in various colleges. He has developed four workbooks which will increase churches' general offerings as well as mission giving.

These books are four- or six-week courses to be taught the weeks prior to the faith promise commitment Sunday.

Growing as a Co-Laborer with God in World Missions

This is a four-week course that will show the giver that he can become a channel of blessing and also receive a channel of blessing back.

The Kindergarten Phase of Eternity

This is a six-week course on the difference between stewardship and ownership. It also shows how to receive commendations from a grateful Lord.

Through the Eyes of Compassion

This is a four-week course that will capture the heart of its reader for lost souls and cause them to first give themselves.

The Great Commission According to Jesus

This is a six-week course that looks at the Great Commission from the four Gospels and the book of Acts. Matthew stresses its authority, Mark stresses the personal need to fulfill it, Luke stresses the true message which will bring repentance, and John stresses the fearful responsibility of each believer. Acts stresses the divine power that is given to the believer.

Guaranteed to increase your mission giving (if done properly) or your money back!

NEW CONVERT CARE
DISCIPLESHIP PROGRAM

These booklets and books are presented to help the layman in the local church. We are dedicated to aiding pastors in strengthening those they shepherd. Through the *New Convert Care Discipleship Program*, we help new converts become happy and active in their church family. Through the *Layman Library Series*, we present books designed to train and strengthen.

Please contact the author for prices.

THE LAYMAN LIBRARY SERIES

A Letter to a New Convert

How to Have Something in Heaven When You Get There

Incentives in Soul Winning

How to Pray so God Will Answer You

Points and Poems by Pearl - Pearl Cheeves

Foreknowledge in the Light of Soul Winning

Elected "To Go"

Predestination Promotes Soul Winning

The Ministry of Paul in the Light of Soul Winning

The Church, a Place of Protection, Love & Development